Seeing True

Ninety Contemplations
in
Ninety Days

By

Ronald Chapman

OZARK
MOUNTAIN
PUBLISHING

PO Box 754
Huntsville, AR 72740
800-935-0045 or 479-738-2348
fax: 479-738-2448
www.ozarkmt.com

Library of Congress Cataloging-in-Publication Data
Chapman, Ronald 1956 -
"Seeing True - Ninety Contemplations in Ninety Days"
by Ronald Chapman
Healing yourself through contemplations in all areas of your life.
1. Self-Help 2. Psychology 3. Rehabilitation
I. Chapman, Ronald 1956 - II. Title

Library of Congress Catalog Number: 2008921737
ISBN: 978-1-886940-80-2

Cover Art and Layout by www.enki3d.com
Book Design: Julia Degan
Book Set in: Times New Roman, Partridge
Published by

PO Box 754 Huntsville, AR 72740
www.ozarkmt.com
Printed in the United States of America

*We seek not just that which is uninjured,
but that within us which is uninjurable.*
-Stephen Levine

To Judy with great love and appreciation.

Introduction

Storytelling may be as old as history itself. At the very least, I suspect it is as old as the history of humanity. With innate connections, wisdom, humor, and sadness, evolution of story cycles ever onward, lifting us to new glimpses of truth, self realization, and compassionate tenderness for each other. Centered for an infinite, precious still moment of time in the lingering cadence of a story, we open our eyes, our ears, our hearts, our very souls to a resonant music irresistibly drawing us to the magnetic north of our true being.

Ron Chapman's collection, *Seeing True: Ninety Contemplations in Ninety Days*, invites us to spend each day in one delicate, thoughtful, time-suspending moment of living story. It is a rare invitation to briefly rest within ourselves and to know, deep within the core of our being, that we are truly divine.

Knowing we are divine is something that tends to happen when you hang around with Ron. To be honest, I don't know exactly how long I have known Ron. It seems like forever, though I know it must be only five or six years. I suspect I am not the only one of Ron's friends who might feel this way. I think the reason is that Ron, in his own forced march through a life of challenges, has survived because he found within himself an infinite reservoir of compassion for the joyous, delightful, totally frustrating, and ever miraculous process of life. These contemplations are each one an exquisite story that elicits, willingly or, yes, sometimes unwillingly, a moment of knowing.

I have two favorite quotes, personal mantras really, that came to my mind as I pondered these contemplations. The first is from Stephen Covey. "Freedom is the ability to pause between the stimulus and the response, and in the pause to choose." Each of these meditations opens a pristine moment of pause. And in that pause the story provocatively prods us to choose. Whatever we choose in that pause, whatever may become real for us in that moment of awareness, be assured the Divine lovingly and safely cradles us.

The second quote is one that I never quite understood when I first encountered it as an English major in college, but it intrigued me with its tantalizing allusion to wisdom. From the poet T.S. Eliot, "We shall not cease from exploration and the end of all our exploring will be to arrive where we started … and know the place for the first time." Wherever your starting point on your own hero or heroine's journey, if you spend ninety days (or more) with these ninety contemplations, you will be embracing exploration, an exploration of your own divine human nature. And the end of that exploring will be in some way to return to the beginning, knowing it again for the first time.

I can't promise you that every moment with these contemplations will be easy, joyous, and calm. But I can promise you that if you let yourself stay with the experience, if you let the threads of story infiltrate your being, if you deeply listen within, you will emerge from these contemplations transformed and renewed. My hope is that you will be ever more connected – to yourself, to those around you, and to the mystical, marvelous mystery of grace. As Ron says, "connecting is our only purpose." In that profound and wondrous connection to Spirit, we can know with a deep sense of gratitude that we are truly blessed.

Lydia Ashanin

Preface

Seeing True is that which lies on the other side of our blindness; and the only path out of blindness is learning to see. While these statements present a dilemma, there is a means by which we can unravel it. In recovery programs, there are many remedies involving action. One in particular is often cited to those who struggle: ninety meetings in ninety days. Everyday sages in these programs say that if you take a specific action for ninety consecutive days, there is a great probability it will take hold in you, become habit and produce change. It is this continuing action that can begin to unravel an addiction.

Similarly concentrated actions can overcome our blindness and thereby allow sight to emerge. But in order to achieve *Seeing True*, we must persistently examine what many spiritual practices call "illusion." People, things, and circumstances are not what we perceive them to be. Reality lies on the other side of those misperceptions. And it is reality which offers us the peace and contentment which we are driven to experience.

Seeing True is a guide and workbook for dispelling our illusions. It contains ninety contemplations, as well as a few simple questions to consider. Ample space is provided for written response. The immediate goals are to create the habit of contemplation, and to produce a small crack in the armor of ego through which deeper understanding can grow.

The long term goal is freedom from the illusions that contract us and limit our lives. We are designed by Life itself to be spiritually fulfilled and lead enriched lives. Anything less is a measure of illusion's grip on us, though it would be foolish to presume that we can define the terms of fulfillment and enrichment. Each of us finds inner satisfaction in our own way. That which pleases me may not please you. In the end, we may even find that our desires for fulfillment evolve or change. We cannot predict the outcome.

The path to freedom begins with contemplation. As illusion's hold on us is weakened through contemplation, we are led to meditation, a quieting process intended to allow the experience of Divine Presence. As meditation quickens the process, we have the opportunity to experience Communion, a deep sense of connection and wholeness. Beyond Communion, the mystics tell us, is the realm of Union. The entire process is one of realization. It is said by some that Union is all we have ever really desired.

But, and this is significant, the path described above is an arduous one. It takes decades to become a master of anything; and it takes a great deal of self-abandonment to embrace that which is offered. So it would be beneficial to immediately abandon the hope that in ninety days we will achieve enlightenment. Instead, consider this a beginning.

Every now and then a river will change course. If you stand upon the bank at the moment of redirection, it appears to be an instantaneous and momentous shift. But to see it clearly, one would have to stand on the bank for decades or even centuries studying the movement of trillions of grains of sand that preceded this dramatic moment.

So it is with us. There are trillions of grains of the sand of self that must be rearranged before we experience a breakthrough. This is the truth, though it runs counter to every bit of popular information to which we are exposed. Sadly, many have come to believe that we can have it all in one minute, find it in a single book, or achieve it through five easy steps.

I suggest a more realistic approach to *Seeing True:* a commitment to a long, slow awakening through a daily practice that begins with a reading to stretch our beliefs and understanding, allows for thoughtful and written reflection and then proceeds to quiet contemplation and meditation. I offer one simple piece of encouragement. What we seek is worth the labor.

Throughout *Seeing True,* I use a variety of names for Spirit, always capitalizing the first letter. This approach is consistent with the desire to overcome our illusions. Most of us

iv

have unconsciously created a fixed concept of a God that is associated with the name we use. This is yet one more illusion we must escape. We can facilitate this by changing the names for It.

Many years ago I went through a period of what I can now acknowledge as profound awakening. For months, every time someone asked me how I felt, I would reply, "It's another day in paradise … it just doesn't look like what I expected."

I can now say I had no idea of the accuracy of that statement. *Seeing True* allows me to know that paradise is already here and now, though it is a far cry from what I imagined. Paradise must be experienced, it cannot be described. What I know of it, I highly recommend. But it still doesn't look like what I expected.

With wonder and love,

Ronald Chapman

Acknowledgements

These contemplations were prepared during a year-long course facilitated by Judy Borich called *AWE*, the acronym for her *Course in Authenticity, Wonder and Expansion*. As this book's dedication suggests, Judy is owed significant credit. So too are those who shared the course with me as well as my mentor, Sam, several teachers, and a host of friends.

Perhaps more important are the people whose stories are included in *Seeing True*. I have been privileged to talk and work with quite a few people in my personal journey. Some of that is presented anonymously, through pseudonyms, or slightly altered in the storyline in order to offer them the consideration they are due for exposing their inner lives to me.

Special thanks to my good friend and fierce but much appreciated critic, David Stalder, for exceptional feedback. Thank you also to my daughter Natalie for much needed final editing. And I am truly blessed by Lydia Ashanin's presence in my life as well as her thoughtful words in the introduction.

Of course, all this is the work of a benevolent Spirit that without exception acts in our best interests. The only response one could offer is gratitude. I am a very fortunate man.

Seeing True

Ninety Contemplations
in
Ninety Days

Spiritual

A small group of men and women came together weekly at the local Jewish community center to talk. Though of many faiths and perspectives, they all shared a common problem of addiction. Each sought a spiritual solution, though each approached it differently.

One evening the dialogue turned to specific spiritual practices, especially meditation. Their experience was quite broad, so the points each made ranged far and wide. The conversation continued, but one man, Bill, did not speak.

After a while someone asked Bill why he was silent. He blushed before saying, "I'm ashamed. I don't meditate. The only thing that quiets my mind is waxing my car."

A hush fell over the group for a long moment before the eldest of the group spoke. "Then waxing your car must be a very spiritual activity."

The discussion shifted instantly to those activities that brought peace to each person. Soon they spoke of the state of inner peace itself.

"But what of joy?" asked one.

Replied another, "Well anything that produces joy must also be spiritual. And that must be true of anything that's good."

Quiet returned before Bill spoke again. "So is sadness not spiritual? Or anger? Or depression?"

A long silence followed. The question needed no answer.

Spiritual - Journal

What brings me peace? In contrast, what agitates me? How do I view these, and what do they mean to me spiritually?

_____

_____

_____

_____

_____

_____

_____

_____

_____

_____

_____

_____

_____

Now

I was sitting in my favorite coffee shop savoring a chocolate bar and a cup of coffee, but not just any chocolate bar and coffee. This chocolate was seventy-seven percent cocoa, and the coffee was decaffeinated Kona brewed extra strong. I was in ecstasy.

For some reason my thoughts wandered to the coffee plantation in Hawaii. It was a different time there with a different angle to the sun, and breezes unlike the southwesterly winds of New Mexico blowing across this high desert. The coffee growers and laborers were eating lunch rather than a late afternoon snack. Coffee beans there languished in a tropical setting, as fruit trees thrived in our dry climate … all precisely at the same moment.

An insight burbled up. It is *now* there just as it is *now* here.

Our perception is profoundly egocentric. We think our particular slice of life is *now*, forgetting that at this same instant throughout the universe there is only one *now*. Granted there are many vantage points, but only one *now*.

Worse, we insist on carving reality into past, present, and future. In truth it is an infinite series of expressions of *now*. There is nothing but *now*.

As I write in this moment seated on an airplane, there is a child sitting a few rows in front of me staring backward. Directly in front of me sits a man with a small bald spot at the crown of his head. The child cannot see the bald spot. Beside the man is a woman who has, at best, an oblique angle of the bald spot. In Atlanta, our destination city, there are people who don't know that this moment includes this man, much less his bald spot.

In my mind an amused voice asks, "Do you promise to contemplate the *now*, the whole *now* and nothing but the *now*?"

Now - Journal

Considering this moment and whatever is right in front of me, what other variations of now can I conceive? Given these many slices of now, what limits my ability to see from this larger vantage point?

Witness

The radio interview ended. It had been a heartwarming conversation about cultural differences and the processes whereby we become acculturated. It was not however some lofty, intellectual discussion, but a gentle, story-like chat.

In the conversation that followed the interview, the guests asked the radio host about the nature of his work. He launched into a description but very quickly lapsed into silence. After a few moments he resumed, "I've never spoken of it this way, but I bear witness to the Divine in others."

Our lives present the opportunity to bear witness. Looking past the challenges or suffering of others, even beyond their successes and joys, we can seek the presence of Spirit in them. It lies beyond the story of our lives, larger and richer than any of us imagine. One sage calls it "the Christ." New Thought spiritual traditions use the word "namaste" to describe it.

Yet it is more than words. It is knowingness, an ability to see and acknowledge the indwelling Spirit animating each of us. To bear witness to the Divine is to see with clarity, and through that sight, to acknowledge Spirit.

Witnessing is simple interaction, like the story a man told of standing in line at a register in a grocery store. He was acquainted with the cashier, but noticed she was particularly radiant that day. "You're more beautiful than usual," he said with a smile.

The woman beamed, or perhaps it is more accurate to say Spirit beamed in response to acknowledgment.

Witness - Journal

To whom have I recently borne witness of the Spirit within? What did I see? If I haven't done so, how might I?

Objectification

There is one pattern of memories that seems to retain its effect: pain at the ending of significant relationships. I remember being devastated when my first wife left me. I sat at the head of the stairs sobbing for Melanie, my two dogs clenched to my chest. With Regina, my beloved second wife, profound grief came as a deep, dark depression. Bewilderment and disbelief describe the ending of my time with Jane, the woman I thought was my life partner after two divorces.

My problem is a human one. We equate love with a relationship, a person, a kiss or sex. In our minds we objectify, mistaking the symbols of love and love itself. In an even more subtle objectification, we convince ourselves that the feeling of love is the love. When we lose the feeling, the relationship, or the embraces, we are disappointed, fearing love is lost.

This is our challenge: to see past objects and concepts, understanding love is permanent, infinite and unyielding. So too with all that matters.

Abundance is. In misunderstanding, we equate it to money, material goods, or financial assets. Yet supply is infinite and cannot be limited.

Well-being is. Since we are the expression of the Divine, as are all things, there is nothing but well-being. Our pursuit of health and happiness demonstrates our confusion.

Spirit is. But we confine the Divine to institutions, philosophies and morals. Rest assured, Spirit far exceeds our conceptions, rules or organizations.

When we gaze upon a rose bush in the middle of winter, it is easy to see the absence of roses. But concluding we have lost roses is failing to see the truth that spring will reveal.

Objectification - Journal

In my daily affairs in worship, relationships, work or play, how do I take that which is and mistakenly translate it into a form, a concept or an object? What consequences result from my misperception?

_____

_____

_____

_____

_____

_____

_____

_____

_____

_____

_____

_____

Large

There was a man who worked at a small car lot. Generally, it was an uneventful experience for him with one notable exception. There was a Mexican man who kept the cars immaculately clean, often uttering simple statements in broken English that could be quite profound.

One day the men were chatting as they leaned against a car. The salesman told his Mexican friend that he was worn out after a busy day. Without missing a beat the worker replied, "Yes ... a very large day."

The man laughed delightedly when he told me the story. I immediately related another tale to him.

I have a friend who has an eight year old son. Without fail, no matter what activities they do on the days they spend together, his son always says, "Dad, this is the best day ever!"

Should we choose to examine our lives, very likely, each of us would find that we are in fact living large. Further consideration would show that were it not for the suggestions of our culture telling us what we lack and where we fall short, we would see our lives in a much different light.

I remember my youngest daughter, Brianne, coming to me with a complaint. Her mother and I were unwilling to allow her as a high school student to spend spring break in Cancun. She told me with tears in her eyes, "I'm the only kid in school who's never been to Cancun."

Large - Journal

Take a few moments to list the events of the day. What do they tell me about the size of my life? Do I have lack? Who told me that I lack?

_____

_____

_____

_____

_____

_____

_____

_____

_____

_____

_____

_____

_____

Detachment

David had been quite troubled, and came to me to try and get some relief from his obsessive thoughts. I listened to him … and I continued to listen. He had relationship troubles.

Finally, he asked me what I thought of his difficulties. I told him gently, "It's not about you."

He looked at me quizzically.

"David, Donna is simply being Donna … perfectly Donna. The problem is that you insist on making it about you."

He stared blankly, clearly not understanding the point.

I continued. "Some years ago before Regina and I divorced, we were in a therapy session. She was describing some situation related to me and I interjected."

Regina was furious. "Damn it, Ron, can't you ever let something be about me?"

I turned quickly to the counselor. There was twinkle in his eyes. He smiled and said softly, "Regina's right."

I gazed at David and smiled. "We're self-centered. We think everything is about us. We have little ability to allow others their experiences without somehow relating it back to us."

My friend grins at me and nods. "Detachment …" he says with clarity.

"Yes," I reply, "detachment. It's not about us. Or as a very wise friend once told me, 'Ron, you'll find your life to be much easier when you're able to stop worrying about what others are thinking about you; and the trick is to realize that most of the time they are not thinking about you at all.' "

Detachment - Journal

How self-centered am I? Am I able to simply be present with others? How do I make it about me?

_____

_____

_____

_____

_____

_____

_____

_____

_____

_____

_____

_____

_____

Courage

There was a spiritual retreat in the mountains east of Albuquerque. It included almost twenty people, all of them seeking something beyond themselves and the difficulties of their lives.

Several people shared during the course of the day. One man's father was on his deathbed; another man contemplated the first anniversary of the death of his wife. A woman recounted her recent near death, an experience which shook her to her core. Others described challenges of every imaginable type including one commenting about thoughts of suicide.

There was a great deal of laughter as they spoke, laughter accompanied by tears of joy.

Life is a courageous act. This is true no matter the outcome, whether seemingly positive or negative. It is true, whether we survive our challenges or not.

When we see the truth ... of life ... that it is filled with difficult scenarios and everyone is living courageously, the feelings that arise are admiration and compassion. When we see the truth, that there is no conceivable failure, we might find we feel peace and joy. When we see the truth, that the actions of our fellows are filled with bravery, we will come to love and appreciate them. When we see the truth, that our lives overflow with courage, we will be struck with awe and wonder.

Life is a courageous act, and we are filled with courage. That's the truth, whether we know it or not.

Courage - Journal

What courageous acts have I taken this day? What courageous acts have I seen in others today? What is the source of that courage?

_____

_____

_____

_____

_____

_____

_____

_____

_____

_____

_____

_____

_____

Laughter

Sitting in a restaurant one evening, I watched an Hispanic family dining. It was an extended family with multiple generations. There was much laughter and gaiety. It was a joy to watch. As a matter of fact, I participated vicariously, much to my own delight.

Many years ago, a wise man told me that the Buddha would routinely sit beneath the bodhi tree and laugh without cause or purpose before settling into his meditations. I decided to adopt the Buddha's practice as an experiment.

What I learned from this laughing practice was more than I imagined. First, I experienced release from my self-imposed dramas. It's very hard to be deadly earnest while you are laughing. Second, I learned that the greatest challenge is learning to laugh at oneself. Third, I discovered that the world does not appreciate when we laugh at situations that are commonly agreed to be important. It's considered subversive.

While forced laughter is hardly authentic, in the end it led to real laughter and the most important lesson of all. In order to see anything in its true light, it is necessary to see it with humor. It's a sure sign that we are not taking it or ourselves too seriously. That is a measure of well-being, as noted by all the spiritually wise men and women who can laugh so readily.

I offer one word of caution however. Others may not want to see the cause of our laughter. Thus we must choose our behavior carefully.

Regardless, try not to take it too seriously.

Laughter - Journal

When am I most likely to laugh? How does it feel at those times? What might it say about how and what I am perceiving?

_____

_____

_____

_____

_____

_____

_____

_____

_____

_____

_____

_____

Being

In recent years, there seems to have been much said in spiritual and personal development circles about being. Often it is in the framework of being-rather-than-doing, accompanied by phrases such as, "I'm a human being not a human doing."

Another common trick is in rearranging our perspective from "Do-Have-Be" to "Be-Do-Have." As it is usually explained, we think we must do something such as write a book in order to have income by which we can then be contented. In contrast, it is proposed we should be satisfied, then do whatever we wish while knowing what we need and want will naturally follow.

There is mischief in these ideas, for they confuse our role in life. Just as we think we are the "do-er," we can readily fall into thinking we are the "be-er." This is simple misperception. We are the vessel. It is Source that does whatever is done. So too does Source be through us.

An old Sufi idea says it quite well. First I thought I was the dancer. Later I thought I was dancing. Finally I found I was being danced.

The mischief of humanity is thinking we are separate from Source, that we think we are a "we." Yet there is only One. It is an infinite Source with infinite expression in an infinite journey. All are manifestations of a single "Be-ing."

Being - Journal

What would Source have me be? This is not to be confused with what might be done, such as a profession or a task. Rather, what is Source's expression and journey through me?

_____

_____

_____

_____

_____

_____

_____

_____

_____

_____

_____

_____

_____

Feelings

When the spiritual path first came to me, I was ignorant of my feelings. I was also frightened by their stirrings. With professional help, I discovered I was in a nearly perpetual state of anxiety, a condition about which I was blind.

The circumstances of my life required me to begin feeling. I could not grow without doing so. But the initial feelings seemed like they would sweep me away. Those feelings had turned into a vast lake grown behind a dam of denial and resistance. As the first trickles began to flow, I feared it would become a raging and dangerous torrent. I had to learn special skills to cope. Slowly, emotions from my past were released and I grew into my feelings. I learned to feel them and to name them. Most importantly, I came to fear them no longer.

I was shown that my feelings are a touchstone to reality, a reliable indicator of who and where I am. Properly understood, I discovered that our emotions are a reliable guide and a sure path to the Creator. But I found that the routes they often choose are unexpected ones. I would need to learn to trust them.

Feelings are valuable in two ways. First they tell us when we have gone astray, falling into self-sufficiency or agnosticism. These are known as fear, anger, frustration, bitterness and their kindred emotions. Most are viewed as bad, though they are actually perfect indicators for when we need to realign ourselves. These are gifts of correction.

Second are the more positive emotions such as love, compassion and joy. These are indications of harmony, the gifts of alignment.

Feelings, once experienced and understood, are the Creator speaking.

Feelings - Journal

What do I feel now? Are there feelings that predominate in my life? Breathe into them and notice what emerges. What do they tell me?

_____

_____

_____

_____

_____

_____

_____

_____

_____

_____

_____

_____

_____

_____

Disquiet

It is troubling to awaken to inner disquiet, then to realize that for unknown reasons the entire night's sleep was filled with it. In fact, my immediate reaction this morning is fear. It seems I have often been frightened that something is amiss within or around me.

Regardless, I arise for a morning walk. In motion, I mentally scroll through all the "disses" with which I've had so much experience, testing each one to see if it fits ... discontented ... discouraged ... disenchanted. Frankly, the length of the list itself is disquieting. I chuckle to myself, which is always a good sign.

I'm caught up in a routine with which I'm quite familiar, attempting to identify and solve a problem. But on this occasion I remember to ask for assistance. "Please God, I need some help."

A few moments later it occurs to me that I'm exhausted, tired of trying to tackle this problem. I'm not just weary from this episode, but from a lifetime of the routine. I've slogged through far too much of my life.

"I quit," I tell myself, though certainly it is a prayer. I decide to settle into the feelings for as long as it takes for them to resolve themselves. I'm just no longer willing to battle. Instead, I breathe into them.

Within a few steps, the disquiet quiets. It's not gone, but I'm no longer exacerbating a feeling that has no apparent cause and certainly no cure. I know this because none of my solutions have ever worked. That's today's insight.

"I quit."

Disquiet - Journal

When have I most recently felt disquiet, discouragement, discontent or their many kindred? What have I done to try to solve them? Has it worked?

_____

_____

_____

_____

_____

_____

_____

_____

_____

_____

_____

_____

_____

_____

Love

Deep in contemplation, I sit, thoughts passing through my mind.

The cold I've been battling is seven weeks old, and I'm tired of it. My neck hurts from a cough-induced whiplash. And I've sprained my ankle, which throbs.

If I am to love anything, I must love everything.

There was a difficult encounter with a friend two days ago. Another friend has been in and out of a crack addiction several times this week. During the workshop I led yesterday, I got so caught up in myself that I offended a participant. Dad was in the hospital again

If I am to love anything, I must love everything.

I am overwhelmed by client demands, fearful that I cannot meet their needs. Those I mentor have asked a lot of me this week.

If I am to love anything, I must love everything.

I feel an inner shift. I breathe into it.

Warm feelings wash over me: a fondness for Beth, a new acquaintance, arises, she is full of light but not yet aware; a gentle compassion slips in for Bill, who struggles, and with whom I have struggled of late; Alicia is a delight, an adept student and steady presence; there are thoughts of Sam, my mentor, who I love as much as I have ever loved anyone; beloved daughters, Natalie and Brianne, fill me with appreciation; and teacher Judy, who has buoyed me lately with deep feelings of gratitude, bubbles into my awareness.

Suddenly, even my health and life challenges are cast in a different light. *I do love everything ... all of it ... madly and deeply.*

Love - Journal

Whom or what do I love? Is there anyone or anything that I cannot or will not love? What is the source of my resistance?

_____

_____

_____

_____

_____

_____

_____

_____

_____

_____

_____

_____

_____

_____

_____

Basking

A friend recently returned from a Caribbean vacation. We agreed to meet at a local New Mexican restaurant. Over enchiladas and carne adovada, she described the delight of basking on the sunny, sandy beaches.

As she described her experience, complete with sensations, I was catapulted into my own memories of another form of basking. Tickled with her and likewise with my thoughts, I shared them with her.

Beyond the realm of prayer, which some consider to be asking something of the Divine, and even beyond contemplation, the careful consideration of spiritual or philosophical matters, is the practice of meditation. On one level it is becoming settled, often in a seated position. On another level it is the observation of thoughts or the machinations of the brain. And perhaps, with practice, it is about stilling the mind.

But beyond these there is what the mystics call communion or union. Some might say we experience oneness or harmony. For me it is a rich experience, a feeling of basking in Presence. It is conscious contact with Source. More than this, it is a place of rest. It is the only time in my life that I am ever able to fully relax.

It comes infrequently, of its own accord, but basking is all I ever sought.

Basking - Journal

When, where and how am I able to feel complete inner quiet? If I can't, what prevents it? Am I willing to move beyond the impediments?

_____

_____

_____

_____

_____

_____

_____

_____

_____

_____

_____

_____

_____

_____

Illusion

A man I know has been immersed in a study of *The Course in Miracles*. He often asks me about concepts that he questions, because he knows I've studied the *Course*.

One day he came to me troubled by the idea that this world is an illusion. Only a few days earlier I heard a master from a different discipline explain this very idea. He said that though the world is real, what we see is an illusion of the real. We see through our perception, which includes distortions since we do not all see, feel, taste, touch, smell or intuit in exactly the same way. Furthermore, everything that comes to us is filtered through our understanding and beliefs. Usually, each of us only has one vantage point from which to perceive that which is real.

The problem is exacerbated by the stories we tell to explain what we perceive. Our personal tales are charged with emotion from experiences that we may or may not be interpreting accurately.

I encouraged him to try an experiment and to gather a handful of his fellow students of the *Course* to observe something. Then each of them should describe what they saw, and more importantly what it means to them.

I was taught long ago that when something appears the same from every possible angle, we are probably seeing reality.

Illusion - Journal

Looking at some situation or circumstance, what do I perceive? Are there other possible explanations?

Reawakening

Sam's merriment caused me a moment of consternation, though I certainly enjoyed hearing his deep, belly laugh. I'd just told him that I remembered the suggestion of a teacher we both held in mutual esteem. The teacher said that a good time for Self-remembering was each time you went to the bathroom.

Sam said demonstratively, "Ron ... it was me who told you to consider Self-awakening every time you go to pee!"

I flushed in embarrassment, then laughed along with Sam. We went on to discuss the importance of what Sam had long referred to as "graciously reawakening as often as possible."

The human state includes a propensity for being mesmerized by the world. We simply forget who we are. We fall asleep.

So a primary goal of any spiritual practice must be Self-remembering. We must reorient ourselves to our True Identity over and over again. The best suggestions seem to lead us to a brief interval of quietude followed by a few moments in Presence.

When we begin practicing, we will find it to be quite difficult to remember to do it. That's a state of mesmerism. We have forgotten.

Then we may likely notice we can remember the need for the practice, but are reluctant to retreat from the adventures of the day.

Eventually, with practice, we will come to see the value of Self-remembering. Sometime thereafter, it becomes as important as remembering to eat ... and yes ... to pee.

Reawakening - Journal

How often have I been able to Self-remember today? Am I willing to practice? Why or why not?

_____

_____

_____

_____

_____

_____

_____

_____

_____

_____

_____

_____

Grace

A few years ago there was a story about two men who nearly lost their lives in Lake Erie. It was a warm summer day. They rode their wave runners out into the lake so far they could no longer see the shore. Then they ran out of gasoline.

The men spent the balance of the day and a long and frightening night in the water. As daylight came both were beginning to succumb to hypothermia. Even though it was summer, the cold water drained heat and life from them.

A short time later a Coast Guard Cutter passed near them. A seaman happened to spot them though they were low in the water and the angle of morning sunlight made it very difficult to see.

After their brush with death, one of the men said, "God sure was with us when they found us!"

This is what many call grace ... an undeserved gift.

But are we then to presume that grace occurs only with the coming of the seemingly good? What of the apparently bad?

Was not God with them even as they rode their craft out into Lake Erie? And did God desert them when they ran out of fuel? What of the long night? Even had they perished, wouldn't God have been as present in their seemingly unfortunate death as in their survival?

Perhaps it is all good ... all grace. Perhaps everything is only appearance, and our attachment to the seemingly good prevents us from seeing true.

Grace - Journal

What do I believe about grace? What of misfortune? Or good fortune? How does the Divine appear in these?

_____

_____

_____

_____

_____

_____

_____

_____

_____

_____

_____

_____

Lottery

There is a comic strip, "Agnes," written by Tony Cochran. It is the continuing tale of a quirky little girl and her odd and enlightening experiences.

In one series, Agnes is lamenting her poor fit in the world. Her friend replies, "A good puzzle has many pieces. You fit in fine!" Agnes is surprised and responds accordingly. The friend speaks again, "Sure! You're the moody, weird girl who has big feet and says odd things." The next frame shows Agnes in quiet contemplation, obviously not knowing what to think of this description.

In the final frame Agnes replies, "I suppose I should feel lucky that I was even included in the puzzle." This draws the punch line, "Yeah! And be glad you're not just another boring piece of sky."

The cartoon instantly sent me back a few weeks to an Italian restaurant in Boise, Idaho, as my friend, Ferd, shared an idea which had struck him.

"Have you ever thought about how we came to be here?" he asked.

I listened as Ferd related his thoughts. Out of a seemingly infinite universe and who knows how many planets, there is the earth. Of all the people here, our parents came together. In a particular moment of lovemaking, one of millions of sperm found an egg. From that hypothetically small possibility, came a unique human being. Thereafter, any number of chance encounters with circumstance and people, everything from potentially fatal viruses to our neighbor next door, have allowed us to be in this moment.

Ferd laughed, "Doesn't it make you think you've won some grand, cosmic lottery?"

Lottery - Journal

What can I identify as the causes of this moment for me? How does this recognition make me feel?

_____

_____

_____

_____

_____

_____

_____

_____

_____

_____

_____

_____

Behaving

The hallmark of enculturation is the process whereby each of us is taught to behave. Early in our life, we encounter a set of standards and expectations established to guide our actions. The process, which teaches us to behave, works by rewarding conformance and punishing deviance.

These guides may be called morals, ethics or philosophies, but their ideal purpose is the alignment of our behavior in ways that help us to thrive.

Yet these behavioral standards also cause much mischief, in no small part because we forget that behavior itself is nothing more than an indicator of intent. Thus we spend our energy trying to improve our conduct without realizing it is not behavior that is the problem, rather it is the source of that behavior, or the intent, wherein the challenge lies.

When our inner state is right, there is no need to control actions since behavior simply falls into line with that inner state. Learn the real meaning of love, and we will act loving without fail. Try to act loving without a loving inner state, and we will constantly fall short. Come to understand the nature of forgiveness, and we will always act in a forgiving fashion. Find compassion within, and all our deeds will be compassionate. Know inner abundance, and we will readily demonstrate charity in all we do.

Some believe we can act our way into right thinking. There is no real evidence of the validity of this idea, and the problem does not lie in our actions. Thus the solution cannot be in behaving.

Behaving - Journal

How do I try to behave? How do I ask others to behave? What is the source of this desire for correct behavior?

Play

A man and his son walked around the corner of the child care center and headed down the breezeway toward the playground. Though the father was quite tall and walked with long strides, the two year old boy leaned forward in anticipation and fell into a toddling near-jog that quickly propelled him well ahead of the man.

Arriving at the edge of the sandy area, the little boy made a beeline to the nearest wooden structure and was instantly absorbed into the flow of other playing children. He climbed the apparatus and within moments was chattering excitedly with two little girls. He was without pretense, drawn by nothing more than the joy of play.

As I watched from the shade of a live oak tree, I remembered a long ago conversation with a friend. We were speaking of the natural human state, and my friend said, "We were born to play ... to act without purpose."

Back in the moment, watching the little boy, I saw the accuracy of my friend's observation. As children, without a plan or agenda, we could knock on a friend's door armed with nothing more than a simple phrase, "Can you come out and play?"

What followed would most likely be total improvisation based on time, place and circumstance. Without an expected outcome or even a design, life would flow through us. And we would play ... act without purpose. Or perhaps it would be more accurate to say that play would happen because we were free from purpose.

Play - Journal

How long has it been since I asked someone, "Do you want to play?" When is the last time I allowed freeform expression in my life?

Gray

I was coaching a young woman recently who was quite frustrated by circumstances in her workplace. She said to me, "Damn it … I want a 'yes' or a 'no!' I'm a black and white type of person. I hate gray!"

I chuckled, not at her, but at a memory of having said almost the same thing many years ago to my mentor. "Ron," he said, "you need to get your colors straight. What lies between black and white is every other color, not gray."

Frankly, I recall being angry that my mentor did not take my frustration seriously. I felt criticized.

Yet the simple truth is that black and white, or the realm of nothing but right and wrong, omits all the glorious possibilities between them. Since Spirit obviously prefers diversity, as evidenced by the world around us, dogmatic beliefs are inconsistent with the nature of things. It is hardly surprising that such dualism creates intolerant, judgmental people, whose most likely contribution to the world around them is condemnation.

It is a tremendous challenge to refrain from seeing only right and wrong, black and white. But it is a key to spiritual development.

An open mind is a mind free from such absolutes. That freedom can welcome God in every imaginable form.

Gray - Journal

What is my sense of right and wrong? How attached am I to it? What is the effect of my attachment to my own life and the lives of others?

_____

_____

_____

_____

_____

_____

_____

_____

_____

_____

_____

_____

_____

Mistaken

Some years ago, a friend showed me what he called the holiest place in New Mexico. It was a grotto tucked into a canyon on the western slope of the Sandia Mountains just outside of Albuquerque. He had discovered it decades before on a day hike. On that day, he was grieving the loss of a relationship. The hike had cleared away much of the clutter of his mind. When he found the grotto, complete with ancient etchings in the rock, he sat down to snack and rest. He wouldn't tell me about the nature of what occurred, but it was clearly a peak experience.

It reminded me of a peak experience I had with a former lover. Actually there were several such occasions in making love with her when the sense of connection was overwhelming. We would pause during sex to feel the incredibly powerful pull between our hearts. It was enough to make us weep.

The similarities between the grotto and the lovemaking run much deeper than just that of the peak experience. My friend and I were both significantly mistaken. He believed his special place in the Sandia wilderness to be sacred ground. I projected the same misunderstanding on my partner.

Certainly what my friend and I felt was holiness, but it is not the place or the person that is holy. We confused the experience of the Divine with a cave and a woman. We forgot that everything is sacred because the Divine which embodies it is sacred, not the form itself. Thus we worship the form rather than the Creator.

Peak experiences are signs of the sacred, but they are not the Source.

Mistaken - Journal

What persons, places, situations and things have I mistaken for the Divine? How did I come to see the form as sacred, rather than seeing the sacred in the form?

_____

_____

_____

_____

_____

_____

_____

_____

_____

_____

_____

_____

_____

Relationship

Joe Bankhead is a wanderer. A former Mormon, he sold his business a number of years ago and now travels the desert Southwest in his little Chinook camper. Joe trusts his heart to provide direction on the road, sells paintings as a means of income, plays chess with anyone he finds who's up for a game, and publishes a monthly journal of his experiences.

In truth, Joe's outer trek is nothing but a reflection of an inner journey. He is quite wise and a full-time seeker of truth, which he finds everywhere he goes.

One evening, as he sat over a plate of enchiladas at Albuquerque's Frontier Restaurant, Joe came to a very profound observation. He asked, "Doesn't the idea of a personal relationship with God imply that everyone's experience of the Divine will be unique to them?"

A very long pause followed and a notable Presence crept into the restaurant. Joe laughed in his characteristically deep fashion. Then he answered his own question. "Of course! And that's why no one can adopt another's idea of God and why dogma of any kind can't suffice."

Relationship is unique to the two parties in relationship. While there will be similarities, no one else will have that exact experience. No one can tell another person what that relationship is like. And no one can insist that their experience is the right one or the only one.

A relationship with Spirit can only be as each of us understands and experiences it. There can be no other.

Relationship - Journal

What do I know about God based on my experience and understanding? What have I adopted from others? What have I attempted to foist upon others?

_____

_____

_____

_____

_____

_____

_____

_____

_____

_____

_____

_____

_____

_____

Song

There is a story told of the songbird. It's said that the bird does not sing to carry a message, but simply because it has a song.

In a world desperate for meaning and seeking purpose, it is foreign to think that we do not need to find or create it, but only express that which is already there. The secret to living abundantly is simply to begin pouring forth, to sing the song whatever it may be.

For many years I marveled that the budgeting process I used always resulted in sufficient income for projected needs. It never fell short. At some point I realized it worked because of the principle embedded within it.

The promise of Spirit is that whatever we may give without demand or expectation will be replenished. Often that which replaces will be greater still than that which has been given. The secret is that it must pour forth in the same way as the bird's song.

The hardest part of this notion is that in order for our lives to be a song, we must be stripped of all the messages we think we bear. We must forfeit intentions, reasoning and justification, and simply throw back our heads and sing.

We must seek to be the instrument upon which the note may be sounded. When ready, the note will be provided. It will not be ours but that which is provided by Source. Be assured, it will be glorious.

Song - Journal

What might be the song I sing? More importantly, what now stands in the way of it being sung?

Fear

For several hours Jonathan and I had been working through his personal self-assessment, an inventory of himself and his challenges. Though he was very tired, the kind of weariness that only an emotional purging can produce, he still wanted to chat about his fears before we finished. So for a short while he cataloged them for me. When he was finished, he asked me what I thought.

I was very quiet for a few moments, listening for the still, quiet voice to speak to me so I might speak to him. Then it came. "Jon, every fear is agnostic."

The line of his jaw tightened. If anything, Jonathan was certain of his love for God. Any suggestion of a lack of faith was guaranteed to produce a negative reaction. Perhaps that is why it needed to be said.

"But aren't there healthy fears?" he asked. "Like fear of being killed, or injured, or of someone else being harmed?"

I looked at him very gently and shook my head. "Jon, on the spiritual level, there is no such thing as harm. That's what was implied when Jesus spoke of turning the other cheek. The only way possible to offer up another cheek is to know there is no harm that can be done."

He began to cry. I sat with him.

After a while he spoke very quietly. "I have been so afraid of the harms I've done to others ... so afraid."

"There's the mistake," I told him. "That self-importance must go. It's causing far too much fear. And fear is just not an option for you anymore."

Fear - Journal

What do I fear? What aspects of self-reliance does it suggest?

_____

_____

_____

_____

_____

_____

_____

_____

_____

_____

_____

_____

Prayer

The men's prayer group met for more than a year. Every Thursday night they came together to support each other in their respective spiritual journeys. While there were many prayers uttered, the most profound action came every week from the same man.

Darren was born simple. There is probably a medical term for what occurred to him before birth, but the result was marginal intelligence and limited emotional development. He worked on a city maintenance crew and lived at home with his parents, though he was approaching thirty years of age.

Each week, Darren would decline to pray for anything. Even when others urged him, he would politely refuse. One evening Darren added to his refusal. He said, "Everything is fine. I don't need to ask for anything."

In the midst of all these men praying for everything from a used car to world peace, Darren knew there was nothing lacking.

A great directive about prayer comes not from any religion but from the world of recovery, from those who say "religion is for those who fear hell and spirituality is for those who have known it." It is their eleventh step which says, "Sought through prayer and meditation to improve our conscious contact with God as we understood Him, praying only for knowledge of His will for us and the power to carry that out."

Such wisdom understands there is no need or lack. It comprehends that the world and everything in it is already in good hands. It recognizes that it is only hubris and arrogance to presume to advise the Divine of what needs attention. It realizes that any perceived need erroneously confirms a lack or fault with the work of God.

Prayer - Journal

For what do I pray? What do I believe is missing or withheld?

_____

_____

_____

_____

_____

_____

_____

_____

_____

_____

_____

_____

_____

Openness

In her book, *A Month of Sundays*, author Julie Mars writes of the search for meaning, for the knowledge of God, and for certainties about life and death. During that search, she has an experience that can only be described as mystical after listening to the life story of Leroy Begay, a Navajo man.

"I skip my afternoon classes and go down to the Rio Grande to work on my sculptures. Every leaf in the cottonwoods shimmers and the black crows that fill their branches look surrealistically huge. When one perches overhead, I look up and say, "Leroy?" (He is in the bird clan.) I sit for hours, higher by far than I have ever been, on the bank of the river ... I still do not know for sure what happened to me. I felt bursting with light, with love, with joy. I felt my cells could not even begin to contain it. Life, my life, that moment—it was supremely perfect in every way. I remained in that altered state for several days ... I was flooded with confidence, with complete certainty, that each individual life, the ups and downs included, is magnificent."

The state Julie describes is openness. It is described by many mystics as well as by those who have studied mystical experiences. Openness comes when the ego yields sufficiently enough for true sight to emerge.

This is the product of Divine benevolence. For some it is instantaneous and unanticipated. For others, it is the result of long hours spent in contemplation and meditation.

Wise men and women who know this openness with sufficient clarity, assure us it is not unique to them. Conscious contact is available to all. As a gift, openness cannot be withheld from those who seek it.

Openness - Journal

What practices bring me closer to Divine contact? If I do not know, what has been suggested by others? Do I practice them?

Free Will

Art had just returned from a walk on the land, a mini-vision quest. He described his experiences in detail, all of which were tinged with the hard edge of self-condemnation. Art had walked and watched, listened and felt. Nothing of significance had appeared either inwardly or outwardly.

The retreat leader sat with an amused smile on her face. Then she asked others in the group what they had heard in Art's tale. The room filled with the most extraordinary observations and insights gleaned from his story.

After a while the leader interrupted and asked Art, "Do you see?" She peered at him intently.

Suddenly, Art was released. He laughed, he wept, and then he laughed some more. Then he said that for the first time in his life, a span of more than four decades, he realized how he viewed himself and his life through judgmental eyes. More importantly, he understood that when the self-critique dropped away, there was nothing but glory.

Art spent a number of weeks in a continuing state of exaltation.

Our culture has adopted various notions of free will. Generally it is an explanatory weapon used to assign self-blame for our failings and suffering.

While there certainly is free will, it is not as we've been led to believe, for there is no blame to be assigned. Instead, free will is the truth that Spirit will always honor our beliefs and perceptions, even if they are amiss. For it is a requirement of spiritual awakening that we see the nature of our misunderstandings.

Art was catapulted out of his misperceptions, only to find that he had been living in grace all the while.

Free Will - Journal

What do I criticize about myself? How do I find fault in others? Do they mirror each other in any way?

_____

_____

_____

_____

_____

_____

_____

_____

_____

_____

_____

_____

_____

Acquisition

In his book, *The Island Within*, anthropologist Richard Nelson describes his decision to live in one place. He chose to never move because of his experiences with indigenous peoples, and explains how many traditional cultures believe that Spirit will provide all things necessary for life and happiness.

Nelson contrasts this with a more modern belief that we must seek out what we desire. The unconscious assumption is that God, gods, or life cannot or will not provide for us. Thus we must somehow acquire what we desire.

A master in another discipline tells entertaining stories about "practical religion." By this he means that many people of religious persuasion profess beliefs in a God or Source that provides, yet do not think it practical for day to day living.

Thus many are driven by an unconscious belief in acquisition. We fear if we do not actively seek out our heart's desire, we shall not receive it.

Teacher and therapist Judy Borich says the spiritual path does not involve getting what we want, but wanting what we get.

For many of us, that idea is an immediate threat, and our troubled response is demonstration of our certainty that if we can only acquire what we desire, then we will finally be happy.

Spirit provides, though not as we might imagine. There is nothing to be acquired.

Acquisition - Journal

What do I seek to acquire? What do these things represent to me? How do I feel about the prospect of not obtaining them? What do I already have?

Wrong

Religion speaks of moral wrong, suggesting we need to become good. It says if we can simply alter our thoughts and conduct from the bad to the good, then our moral problems will be solved.

The medical model addresses the realm of illness, the idea that there is something physically wrong. If we can create wellness to replace the sickness, then matters will be made right.

Therapeutic practices believe how we perceive, feel and experience ourselves, others and the world is the source of wrong. If we can only make right our personal senses of shortcoming, then all will be well.

Some spiritual disciplines identify some or all of our thoughts and thinking as wrong. If we can renounce them, then we will reach resolution.

All these concepts start with a premise of wrongness. They tell us something is amiss. Imagine, we affirm that the universe ... Spirit ... has blundered. And we assume that a proper action can remedy flaws in the creation. Or worse, we imagine that the Divine has or is withholding the correction.

Perhaps there is no wrong to be righted. Perhaps all is perfect. Perhaps we are asleep, deeply and profoundly asleep. Perhaps we need only to awaken and the spiritual dreams and nightmares will simply cease to exist. Perhaps then we will see there is no wrong.

Wrong - Journal

What do I believe is wrong in my life and the world? What remedies do I seek? Do they solve the apparent problem?

Mystical

Every day innumerable creatures die from perfectly adapted and evolved bacteria. Those germs are perfect spiritual expression, imbued with the sacred, and the death they produce is likewise holy. Today, millions of objects manufactured from substances like wood, plastics and metal will fail. In some cases damages will result, whether great or small. Thank God that wood rots, metal erodes, and structures break. Were it not so, we would be living in a permanent clutter of created items. Decay is Spirit in action.

And there are most certainly cataclysms awaiting us. Earthquakes are an essential part of plate tectonics, without which the earth would just be another rock floating in space. Landslides are an inevitable consequence of mountains rising. Tornados and hurricanes are a requirement of weather systems; to eliminate them would require the end of precipitation and much of the world would become desert.

There are also manmade tragedies. On the day men flew airplanes into the World Trade Center, they were labeled terrorists and their acts were called evil. Yet they believed they were living out their highest expression. Spirit embodied those beliefs.

There is nothing that is not Spirit. There cannot be anything without Spirit, or anything that excludes Spirit.

The mystical secret is not a secret. It is within and around us all the time. The secret is in the seeing ... seeing beyond the physical and beyond our perception.

Mystical - Journal

Name someone, something, or some occurrence that seems to exclude Spirit. How might I see it differently?

_____

_____

_____

_____

_____

_____

_____

_____

_____

_____

_____

_____

_____

Passing

My sister and I were present for my dad's passing. Life exited him in waves. The heart monitor flatlined several times, each time rebounding but with decreasing heart rates. A few moments after life finally ebbed away, air began slowly escaping from his lungs. Then he was still.

Deana and I looked at each other with childlike curiosity. "Is he dead?" she asked. With an assuredly goofy look on my face, I shrugged.

Long moments passed as his face grayed. After a while we conceded he was gone. We called the doctors for their concurrence.

We chatted for a while thereafter. I shared my observation that we really don't know what death is. Whether a tree that no longer grows, a deer smashed by a car, or my father, all we can say is that whatever formerly animated them is no longer present. We do not know more than that; all the rest is conjecture.

Before they took Dad's body away, I touched his hair and caressed his forehead. His skin was chilled. Tears welled in my eyes.

In a later e-mail conversation with Stephen Levine, the great student of death and dying, he told me he had caught Dad's spirit passing. He said he felt a great rush of love for me, and a request for my forgiveness.

I don't know what needs forgiving. I don't know where Dad has gone. I don't know what I believe about souls or spirits.

I agreed to begin a practice of forgiveness.

Passing - Journal

Whose passing have I not grieved or mourned? Is there a deed or misdeed in need of forgiveness?

_____

_____

_____

_____

_____

_____

_____

_____

_____

_____

_____

_____

_____

Special

I was caught up in myself, trying to prove that I mattered. I prattled on about what I needed to do to demonstrate my significance.

My friend listened to my ramblings, then looked me directly in the eyes. She said to me, "Ron, let me get this straight. You're trying to show your significance?"

I nodded, not seeing where she was leading me.

She snorted in amusement. "Ron, you're the most accomplished guy I know. Just what would be significant?"

I felt a sinking feeling in my belly as awareness washed over me. I was transported back to a day twenty years before, when another female friend, Maureen, had leveled me in a similar fashion. I had been lamenting that I felt my life to be a loss, that I had done nothing special with it.

Maureen was very gentle in her reply. "You are special, Ron. And so is everyone else."

The Course in Miracles suggests it is our pursuit of specialness that is our spiritual dilemma. We seek to be somehow different from others ... to be special. We may aim to rise above, or to distinguish ourselves, or to be more absurd or uglier in our behavior, but it's really no more than an attempt to be different.

In order to be special, we must reject our Oneness and wholeness. Worse, there is never enough specialness to satisfy our need.

It is fiction to think we could be anything but perfect spiritual expression.

Special – Journal

How do I seek to be special and distinctive? How might this separate me from others and from Spirit?

Sacrifice

Renee knew immediately something more was being revealed. The question she had been asked probed deeper than she had yet been able to see within herself.

Her teacher asked again. "All great spiritual traditions speak of the value of self-sacrifice. Why are you so reluctant to give yourself up?"

After a long pause Renee replied, "I don't know. It just frightens me."

The older woman nodded compassionately. "Sacrifice is filled with mischief. When Jesus spoke of turning the other cheek, he knew there were two conditions necessary to do so. First, you must know in your heart that the person striking you is not harming you, but lashing out from their own injuries and illusions. Second, you must understand there is nothing to defend, that all is well even up to loss of life."

She peered into Renee's eyes before adding, "Do you see? As long as we believe another is doing wrong, or that we must defend ourselves, sacrifice does not come from love but from the self."

Mesmerized, Renee shook her head. There was a brief moment of insight for her, but full comprehension would have to wait for another day.

Sacrifice - Journal

What means of self-sacrifice do I use? Do those methods come from love, or out of mischief?

_____

_____

_____

_____

_____

_____

_____

_____

_____

_____

_____

_____

Children

It's a hot summer's day in downtown Memphis, as a woman enters the central atrium of Peabody Place with her two children. She is smiling and the little boy and girl skip along gaily, each holding one of her hands. She sits and the children begin to explore.

The boy plucks a leaf and brings it to her. She receives it and laughs at the perfect gift. The girl climbs upon a planter. Her mother laughingly calls to her, "Anna, come down from there."

Now the boy is trying to reach into the pool and touch the sculpted ducks that spit fountains of water. Mom snatches him up and playfully swings him away.

At that moment little Anna calls from a platform she has discovered at the top of the stairs, "Mama, I can see the ducks." Her mom looks up and beams at her. "Can you now, honey?" The little girl lights up with a smile.

The boy runs screaming around the patio while the woman chases him. They both laugh. A few minutes later she has bribed them both with fruit smoothies and all three sit slurping noisily.

Across the bridge that bisects the pond rush three more children, grandparents following slowly. The young ones stop in the middle of the bridge. One shouts with delight, "Ducks!" The elders smile as the children race away, screaming and laughing.

The plot unfolds anew.

Children - Journal

What is it to be child-like? Why is it significant?

Esteem

Ellen struggled with her self-image as a result of a troubled and tumultuous childhood that resulted in an eating disorder. From peers in a recovery program, she adopted a mantra: "If you want self-esteem, do esteemable acts." That approach had worked well for some time, but lost its effectiveness. She came again to suffer from inner self-loathing that simply would not yield, no matter what wonderful actions she might take.

Someone told her more was being revealed to her, that she would need to go to greater depths in order to gain relief. She balked. But eventually her discomfort - the gift of pain - caused her to seek new perspectives and assistance. She was led to a spiritual teacher.

Within a very short time, the teacher helped Ellen to see that the problem was not lack of self-esteem, so no amount of esteemable acts could make her feel better. Ellen had to learn there was no "self" to hold in esteem, that there is only Spirit. The appearance of, and belief in, a "self" apart from the Divine was her challenge.

This work brought her to her knees emotionally and psychologically. In order to finally heal, she had to stop attempting to bolster a "self" that was in itself the problem.

She learned to esteem the Divine. Relief came. Slowly and steadily, Ellen's difficulties improved.

Esteem - Journal

What do I hold in esteem about myself? How have I attempted to bolster my esteem? What results has it provided?

_____

_____

_____

_____

_____

_____

_____

_____

_____

_____

_____

_____

_____

Platinum

The facilitators encouraged workshop participants to describe how they wanted to experience relationships in their lives. Almost immediately a woman mentioned the golden rule, "Do unto others as you would have them do unto you." Promptly, another mentioned the platinum rule coined by Dr. Tony Alessandro, "Do unto others as they would have you do unto them."

The group leaders nodded in agreement then shared their story. They were married and had struggled with one long-standing challenge that illustrated the point. He had grown up in a family that gave large gifts at birthdays and Christmas, while her experience had been one of small, personal gifts.

At each gift-giving occasion, she would give a beautiful item but never a large one. It seemed she was sure he would come to appreciate these lovely gifts. But with each gift he felt a sense of disappointment, though he was hesitant to speak of it.

Finally, on one of his birthdays, he cracked. "Damn it! I know it makes no sense. But when I get a big gift I just feel loved."

A few months later at Christmas, there was a massive box for him beside the tree. It was filled with garden tools. He wept with joy.

The hardest thing in the world is to simply give people what they wish, to set aside our desires and cater to their desires. It requires relinquishing part of our "self," which can be a great challenge. But it is holy conduct, for it is to love them as they wish to be loved.

Platinum - Journal

Choose one or several loved ones or friends. How can I act in a way that demonstrates the platinum rule? What impedes me from doing so?

_____

_____

_____

_____

_____

_____

_____

_____

_____

_____

_____

_____

_____

Quiet

I remember a time many years ago when I sat on a petrified log in the Southwestern desert. It was early morning and there was no sound to be heard. It was absolutely quiet: no insects buzzing, no aircraft distantly roaring, no sound of cars or human footfall. Soundless.

I would say of it later, "It weirded me out." I didn't know what to do with all the openness of the quiet. It scared me. A person could get lost in all that silence.

Now, years later, I have come to relish the quiet. Since it is increasingly difficult to find in our world, I have discovered how to find it inside. But it is even easier to get lost in that silence, to be swallowed by it. Yet now the stillness is comforting, a place to feel the beating of my heart and the swell of Spirit that fills me.

At this moment I sit in an airport amid the busyness of human industry. I can feel the hum of it, from vibrating floor to the radiating energy of passing people. Yet while in the world, inner quiet allows me to be not of the world.

Quiet reminds me who I am. It allows space between activities that would incorrectly define me through action and that true part of me which is indefinable by human terms.

In silence there is peace. Or perhaps the silence is peace, all the rest white noise.

Quiet - Journal

Does Spirit have a noise associated with it? Or is Spirit in the quiet? What keeps me from the silence, or draws me to it?

_____

_____

_____

_____

_____

_____

_____

_____

_____

_____

_____

_____

_____

Wanting

It was a difficult discussion for me. As the other members of the group listened, I began to explain my understanding of getting what I need in a relationship.

Before I could complete a few sentences, Judy cut me off. "No." She shook her head vigorously. "The spiritual path is not about getting what you want, but about wanting what you get."

I quickly interjected, "But, what about ..."

She cut me off again. "No. No buts." She looked at me sternly but lovingly. "You don't get a vote on your path."

Once again I attempted to edge in a comment, and she terminated it immediately. "God decides your path. Your choice is to want what you get."

Judy looked at me. I remained silent, allowing myself to absorb her comments. I felt the inner resistance, the voice that insisted that if it wasn't about getting what you want my whole world might collapse.

Timidly I asked, "So what's the point?"

Now she laughed. "Ron," she said sweetly, "there is no point."

Fear shot through me and must have shown on my face, for Judy nodded in appreciation of the dilemma this posed.

I realized that in no small part, this was the principle of acceptance. Circumstances are as they are. My task is not to question them, but to accept them. This presents an opportunity for resolution and real progress. Then and only then can I act with appropriate effect. Then and only then can Spirit lead.

Wanting - Journal

What do I want? Is it other than what I have? What can be done to accept that which is?

_____

_____

_____

_____

_____

_____

_____

_____

_____

_____

_____

_____

_____

_____

Hope

"Perhaps there is a better way," announced the leader.

Her words rang as a message of hope through the group. Those gathered were seekers, and while their quests were as varied as their personalities, each had experienced the reality of human limitation and failure. In fact, the leader had confirmed that the recognition of human inadequacy was a prerequisite for a solution.

The leader proceeded with a series of stories to illustrate. She began with her own tale of addiction from which she had been freed. Then came the story of Lynn who had received relief from chronic back and neck pain. Then there was Owen who was catapulted out of lifelong despair, and Robert, who without physical relief from chronic pain, had nevertheless received a new state of mind that rendered the pain quite tolerable.

Then she spoke of hope, without which many would have perished long ago. She raised herself to her full height with a deep breath, announcing with conviction, "Rest assured, there is nothing that cannot be made right."

And Spirit made an appearance with her words. Many of those in the room visibly relaxed. One man began to cry.

Hope, as evidenced in the stories of others, raised them up. It provided for the possibility that their labors were not in vain, that relief was available, that their sorrows could be remedied.

The leader burst into tears.

Hope - Journal

What brings me hope? And what is it for which I hope?

Upset

"Don't sweat the small stuff," said the older man to his protégée. "And don't forget that it's all small stuff."

I overheard their conversation as I sat in a restaurant in Denver. As much as I tried to not listen to them, I could not resist. While I had heard this advice many times before, it still made me wince.

It is understandable that in relative terms, some issues are of much more immediate or significant concern. But it is spiritual denial to minimize upsets. Any emotional trouble, no matter how seemingly trivial, is an obstacle to the expression of Spirit. When anything produces fear or pain, it is significant, regardless of whether its cause is substantial. Denying it only represses that which is in need of healing. If it hurts, it hurts.

I watched my own inner turmoil as I debated whether to interfere in their conversation and relationship. I breathed into the ache I felt. Soon tears welled in the corners of my eyes. A few memories seeped into my awareness. I felt a sharp pain in my chest as I recalled the denial of sorrow in my own life. Worse were the thoughts of those who had neglected to tend to my pain.

I breathed more deeply, alternating my attention from memories to people and then to feelings. Soon forgiveness washed over me. Healing was complete. My upset ended.

I arose from the table. As I left the restaurant, I offered a generous nod of acknowledgment and encouragement to the older man serving as a mentor.

Upset - Journal

What "small stuff" troubles me? How and why have I denied it? What would it take to be released?

_____

_____

_____

_____

_____

_____

_____

_____

_____

_____

_____

_____

Condemnation

It was an odd experience. My sister and I were in a wide ranging discussion about societal ills and solutions, when I suddenly discovered we were quite far apart on a very important theme.

This was an unusual circumstance. Deana is so knowledgeable on so many things that I was surprised to see I had a perspective that was not one she had considered.

I had commented that my issue with our culture's solutions to social ills was the condemnation of others we so often expressed. I used the example of incarceration as punishment, rather than as a solution. She promptly pointed out that one must judge the circumstances around us, including people.

It was then I saw the disconnect in our reasoning. I realized that Deana did not see one could take action without condemning someone. For example, we can incarcerate someone who is a sexual predator of children without seeing them as evil, but to protect our children. Indeed, the highest spiritual callings seem to move from this vantage point.

The key to a genuinely spiritual perspective of others is to renounce our opinions of them or their behavior - to judge not - while simultaneously recognizing we must still choose some course of action or inaction. Simply, we must act without prejudice from that quiet inner place of non-judgment. We must renounce our condemnation of others, for it has no place in spirituality.

The only path to such a place is to vanquish the fears within ourselves that trigger the condemnation of others.

Condemnation - Journal

What do I condemn in others? What would it take to be free of the need to judge them?

_____

_____

_____

_____

_____

_____

_____

_____

_____

_____

_____

_____

_____

_____

Stripped

Sunny had been quite ill, one of those bizarre infections caused by an otherwise routine bacteria. The illness nearly killed her.

She later described her feelings as she lay in the hospital bed unable to move or speak. As a dancer and visual artist, she had spent her life in motion, making a contribution to the world. Now she was helpless, and there was the very real prospect that she might remain totally dependent.

Sunny described how emotionally difficult it was being unable to even thank those who cared for her. But an even greater pain came from the thought she might never again be able to do anything she loved or that added value to the world and to those around her.

Stripped of everything through which she derived meaning, Sunny was forced to consider her innate value. Could she thrive even if everything of importance was forfeit? Could she find meaning for herself without the ability to act?

It was a torturous situation that clearly demonstrated her dependence on external experience and expression.

Fortunately, Sunny regained much of her ability. But on some level she remained stripped of that which formerly created her identity. And a great sense of appreciation came to her.

What we identify ourselves with can vanish in a heartbeat. If we are not our actions, we are left to contemplate the meaning of our existence and the purpose of our life. Sunny found something beyond outer expression. We must find it too.

Stripped - Journal

On what is my identity based?

Response

Breathe, just breathe. Notice the breath.

Do you know how to breathe?

The simple truth is "no." The millions of electrical impulses needed to contract and expand the muscles of the torso in order to breathe are so complex that if we needed to know how to operate them we would die of oxygen deprivation very quickly.

But we breathe.

An explanation is that deep in our unconscious an intention is held that it would be valuable to breathe. And in response to that intention Spirit breathes through us.

So it is with everything: making love, switching on a light, driving a car, or reading these contemplations. Action flows forth from intention as perfect spiritual expression.

The response occurs as long as we are animated by life; every moment of every day is in fact a perfectly choreographed dance between Spirit in response and Spirit within us stating intention. Spirit engaged with Spirit.

There is great comfort in knowing that every thought, conscious or unconscious, is perfect prayer to which perfect response is offered.

There is great consternation in realizing that any trouble we experience is likewise a perfect response from Spirit.

The only question to be asked is, "What is the intention that produces our difficulty?"

Response - Journal

What difficulties do I face? What might be an intention that produces these difficulties?

Is

"But I'm not being asked for my input," he said. "That's what is!"

"No," I told him firmly, "that is not what is."

Paul looked at me angrily. Not only was he having trouble grasping the point, he was feeling thwarted in his attempt to have his voice heard among his peers, and for Paul, not being heard was a very painful situation.

"Okay," I said. "Let's take the setting and talk about what is. Describe it to me."

Paul took a measured breath to calm himself. "It's a large conference room. There are five architects seated around the table, including me. Lewis has just finished asking everyone but me ..."

I cut him off. "Try that again Paul. Tell me what is, not what isn't."

He sighs, then resumes. "Lewis has asked Connie, David, and Stephanie for their thoughts."

I see he is carefully considering his words.

"I have something to add, and I want to be asked. Lewis doesn't ..." Paul stops as he catches himself. "I sit and listen."

"Good," I reply. "Mischief creeps in whenever we allude in any way, shape or form to something that is not. We seek to make an *is* of an *is not*, and to believe it to be true. But that which *is not* can be nothing more than conjecture ... fiction."

Paul's brow was furrowed as he pondered the point.

"An *is not* is always a charged issue for us, a story that lets us play out our sense of exclusion or injury. That's the mischief," I said.

"Oh," Paul replied. "I was playing victim."

Is - Journal

What is at this moment? Right now?

Separation

Looking down on the Hawaiian islands, there appear to be multiple islands separated by water. But if we were to peer beneath the water's surface, we would discover they are joined.

So it is with the continents; there is an appearance of physical separation. Yet there is equally only one form.

Standing in an apple orchard we see many trees. Were we to pick an apple and eat it, we would perceive the apple as separate from the tree. As we arrive at the core and its seeds, we can see a different reality. The life of the apple tree passes into the apple and seeds. Plant the seed and the same life that was in the tree, which has passed to the seed, becomes the life of a new tree.

There is an appearance of separate lives. Yet there is only one life.

Gazing dreamily into a blazing fireplace on a cold winter's night, we imagine the energy of the fire as separate from the energy of the furnace. Or greater still, we conceive of these energies as apart from the energy of electricity, or wind, or sun. But Albert Einstein posited that all matter reduces to energy. All things, seen and unseen, are nothing but energy.

There is only the appearance of separate energies. There is only one energy.

Is not energy really power?

Perhaps there is only one Power. Perhaps there is nothing but that Power, regardless of appearances.

Separation - Journal

Where do I see separation? How might I see it in another light?

_____

_____

_____

_____

_____

_____

_____

_____

_____

_____

_____

_____

_____

_____

Presence

The young woman stood in front of those assembled to hear her tell of her recent spiritual experience. There was a light in her eyes, but her lightly trembling hands revealed her humanity. She was very animated as she told the tale. Her audience accepted her with open postures, bright smiles, and nodding heads.

She reached the climax of her tale and with arms wide said, "I was so angry I just let God have it, cussed that son-of-a-bitch out." She paused to collect herself.

A hush fell upon the room, though it was not clear if anyone was offended by her anger and cursing, or whether they were simply caught by the power of her tale.

Oblivious to the effect her words were having, she continued. "I remembered someone saying that if my God wasn't big enough to handle my rage, I needed a bigger God ..." She struggled to find the right words. "... and then it struck me ... no, not a lightening bolt." She giggled, "I was overwhelmed by a feeling so big it brought me to my knees. Whatever it was, it was big enough to love me even while I cussed it."

A deep stillness filled the room. Almost immediately a Presence descended. It was so palpable the silence extended for several moments.

The young woman's voice cracked as she spoke again. "There it is again!" She smiled and shook her head in amazement. "It's like when I tell the truth, it always shows up. I can't believe I never noticed it before."

Presence - Journal

When am I aware of Presence?

Choice

"Would you like to choose again?"

Students of *The Course in Miracles* were struggling with the instructor's point. The teacher, Tom, grinned gently and mischievously in response to the obvious consternation filling the room.

Furrows of concentration spread across Audie's forehead as she asked, "Are you telling us we can't choose what we want?"

Tom's face softened. "You can choose whatever you want, but if it's producing discontent or pain, you might want to choose again. Maybe the only choice is to choose peace."

Another teacher explained that the only choice for peace is in choosing that which is presented, to embrace what is here and now. Her words echo those of still another teacher who often says, "Try to choose from those things which are available, rather than those which are not."

The secret to choosing peace comes in understanding that without awareness, there is no choice. This conflicts completely with our culture's perception of choice, or free will, which is used to assign blame for matters gone awry. Most so-called "freedom of choice" is, in fact, compulsive and unconscious behavior.

However, there is innate potential for choice within each of us. It becomes available in response to awareness. Clarity comes from awareness, and when we see accurately, we can choose a path of peace.

Pain is the gift that tells us each time we choose poorly.

"Would you like to choose again?"

Choice - Journal

Do I want peace? What prevents me from choosing it?

_____

_____

_____

_____

_____

_____

_____

_____

_____

_____

_____

_____

Pain

Many years ago when I was a boy, my dog had a close brush with death. She was in the street in front of the house when a car roared over the hill upon which our home perched. The driver slammed on the brakes but couldn't avoid Micki. He hit her just hard enough to send her skidding across the pavement.

The asphalt left Micki with a terrible case of road rash that covered her entire rear end. The result was a painful, long-lasting scab. It proved to be the perfect lesson. The pain and injury were not serious, but the experience was sufficient to keep the dog out of the road for the rest of her life.

The memory of Micki flooded back one day as I listened to an old fellow by the name of Jim Peterson talk about his life. At first, it seemed a tragic tale of D-Day, the long march to Germany and the end of World War II, and the terrible alcoholism that drove Jim insane. His downward spiral ended in a pit in the Kansas State Penitentiary where he awoke one day after a long bout of craziness. He vividly recalled his emaciated condition and fingers without nails, the consequence of malnutrition.

The story he told was not tragic, though his road back was arduous. Instead, Jim spoke of his almost full recovery and the deep and abiding sense of gratitude that resulted.

The most powerful part of his story is life changing in its perspective. "Cuddle up to pain and fear. Make them your friend. See what they have to teach you. You're going to find they're a great gift."

Like Micki, Jim's pain was a life altering factor. It is pain's power to teach that makes it a gift.

Pain - Journal

How do I handle pain? Am I able to embrace it? Can I imagine that it is a gift and be thankful? What keeps me from doing so?

_____

_____

_____

_____

_____

_____

_____

_____

_____

_____

_____

_____

_____

_____

We

It came in a meditation. For the first time in my life, I saw beyond me. In an instant, I realized everything I had done in my life until that moment had been as "I," as that which is separate and apart. A brief glimpse of "we-ness" emerged from that instant, bringing with it a new perspective.

I recalled a mystical account of one who was transported out of bodily consciousness. Suddenly, he viewed the world from the vantage of a leaf on a tree. In retrospect, he said there is only a collective reality; any sense of an "I" is a misperception.

I mentioned the moment to my teacher. She laughed as I described finally getting outside myself. She said, "That would be good, since there is no self."

Since her comment, my experience of "we-ness" has only accelerated. The lines of distinction between me and everything else have blurred. Sometimes it feels as if that which was formerly separate is now merging with me in the same way watercolors bleed into each other as they wash onto canvas. On occasion, I sense the discomfort of the ego, for it is losing its distinction. The perception of a separate self is dissolving.

There is only One. Seeing "we" is a first step toward experiencing it.

We - Journal

Can I see beyond me? Do I see others as separate from me? Do I see the world as apart from me? How does it feel to consider otherwise?

_____

_____

_____

_____

_____

_____

_____

_____

_____

_____

_____

_____

_____

Lover

Deep in the night, I wake. A feeling swells in my chest, lifting me. Fear clutches at my diaphragm for a moment for I do not know this feeling. Yet the feeling is so wonderful I surrender to it.

It radiates outward and upward, pressing my chest higher still. There is reciprocation. I am in love but there is no lover present.

At the edge of my awareness a sexual urge tickles my groin, but vanishes when no energy is directed toward it. Instead, I am swept up in what must surely be the Beloved.

With this realization comes a deeper surrender, and Love envelops me. I relax into it. There is only Presence.

On later reflection, I see I was consciously with God for the first time. It was not a relationship, but a relating ... a verb not a noun ... and completely unconditional.

I see that our "dos" and "don'ts" block spiritual connection. We insist upon behavior and codes to define a relationship with the Divine. So too do our beliefs impede Presence, telling us how It ought to be rather than guiding us to that Being.

Apparently, God does not care what we believe or profess. God only cares that we come into Presence. God knows no separation, for there is no separation. There is only the Lover and loving.

Lover - Journal

What codes, morals, beliefs or practices do I insist upon? Why must they be so for me? How might these impede relating with God?

Attracted

A woman I've known for some time came to me troubled. She was concerned so many women were being attracted to her and the message she had been given. She feared it would overwhelm her. Worse still, she feared she had nothing to give.

I told her the story of Joel, founder of a mystical path. Joel was a salesman, and totally ignorant of God.

One day, a customer came to Joel. The customer asked Joel to pray for him, believing Joel's prayers would heal him. In consternation, but with a surprising degree of open-mindedness, Joel later closed his eyes and prayed for the man. He told God he knew nothing of such matters, but he was willing. The customer was healed. In the course of the next week, Joel was inundated with requests for healing from former customers.

My friend loved the story. I proceeded to offer a number of observations ranging from biblical suggestions like not hiding a light under a basket on a hill, to considering the notion of "attraction rather than promotion" which is central to twelve step programs. Then I suggested that the light was shining so brightly through her she could not conceal it. She balked, not really able to see that in herself. But she agreed to cooperate with what Spirit seemed determined to bring to her.

A few months later, she told me a woman from the East coast had sought her out and was flying to Albuquerque in order to experience what my friend had to offer. She was pleased and a little overwhelmed.

Where Spirit shines, people will see.

Attracted - Journal

Do I promote, or do I allow attraction to take place? Regardless, why do I choose attraction or promotion?

_____

_____

_____

_____

_____

_____

_____

_____

_____

_____

_____

_____

_____

Free

I've had a long-running routine with my spiritual mentor, Sam. I regularly ask him, "What's your purpose today?" While there has been some change in his responses over the years, one phrase has recurred over and over again, "To be free to experience what is."

This continuing conversation about purpose has been an extremely important one for me. Like many people, I have struggled with the meaning of life and even more so with the reason for my existence. It seems I must have a purpose for my life, because the prospect of pointlessness is rather daunting. Fortunately, Sam has been exceedingly patient over the fifteen years of this discussion.

The real test of a purpose is whether it meets the demands of the day. Being free to experience what is has proven to be a daily purpose that really works quite well.

But I must admit there is much that has obstructed my practice of it. There is a constant battle to try to control life, a futile but recurring theme. My opinions and certainties obscure vision and understanding, while also provoking me. Fears and insecurities constantly rise from within.

The only thing that prevents freedom are these inner manifestations. To be free is to release them. But first we must identify and acknowledge them.

Free - Journal

What opinions, prejudices and certainties limit my ability to experience whatever may come?

New

In a class in criminal justice, the professor told a most entertaining story about the now defunct "Just Say No" campaign against the use of illicit drugs. He said, "It's a great program for anyone who is not likely to use or become addicted to drugs. But it's been proven useless to those likely to become addicts."

The ensuing dialogue among the students and the professor was incredibly rich. It revealed there was scant understanding of behavioral problems such as addiction. One participant with a background in recovery work clarified that, "Asking someone with a drug addiction to not use drugs is just about as effective as telling someone with diarrhea to refrain from crapping." That brought a roar of laughter from the students.

The professor added two important pieces of information to the conversation. First, he emphasized that our tendency to view others and their behavior through our personal experience was very problematic. As he stated it, "For me to assume that since I can stop drinking after one martini, that you should likewise be able to do so, is terribly misleading. Some are much more prone to addiction than others."

Then he added that anyone wanting or needing a change required an infusion of something new. "You can't teach yourself, and you can't get it from your peers. Whether it's information or insight, it must come from someplace or someone new to your experience."

The student with the background in drug rehabilitation added, "That's the importance of a Higher Power."

New - Journal

What or who are the sources for new information or insight for me?

Listen

"It's good that you spend so much time helping others," offered the bereaved man to the hospice volunteer.

She nodded. Then after careful consideration, she replied, "I just spend time with people. It's God that does the helping."

Her words echoed those of my mentor who over many years has said time after time that we work with others and leave the outcomes and credit to Spirit. Yet another teacher spoke of "bearing witness to the presence of the Divine."

These recollections slipped through my mind as a woman struck up a conversation with me as we waited on our auto mechanic to complete repairs. She said only a few words before turning to an upbeat story in the morning newspaper and reading it to me. She beamed in response to the tale's outcome.

I listened as she spoke of the house she was building with her boyfriend. She bemoaned the huge nail that had flattened her tire that morning and brought her to the auto service center. Then she spoke of her job recruiting nurses to tend elderly patients with chronic health problems. It was not the perfect job, if there even is such a thing, but it made her feel good.

She introduced herself as she rose to leave and meet her boyfriend, who had come to take her to work. We said goodbye.

I listened, though I know not for what purpose, if any. I simply bore witness. I shared a few moments with her.

I did nothing.

Listen - Journal

To what or whom do I really listen? Why do these hold my attention and interest?

_____

_____

_____

_____

_____

_____

_____

_____

_____

_____

_____

_____

_____

Indulgence

One of the most fun interactions I have with audiences occurs when we indulge in ourselves. I ask them to tell the stories about themselves that fill them with pleasure.

This is a very subversive activity. After all, most cultures do not encourage nor easily accept such indulgence. It is seen as self-absorbed.

But as I once heard someone say, "I don't think much of myself, but I'm all I think about." There is accuracy in that statement.

So I suggest to audience members that we should simply stop the deceit. I ask them to say out loud, "Enough about you, let's talk about me!" Inevitably, that gets the laughter flowing.

Because they are so often reluctant to speak of their delight in themselves, I often must kick start the process by sharing about myself. But once participants get underway, it's interesting to see how much fun they have. And often, self-consciousness drops away. The result can be a presence of Spirit that fills the room and everyone present.

There is a secret in this self-indulgent behavior. It is the principle of being "right sized," which some might call humility.

Each of us is a mix of attributes, some of which may have positive outcomes and some negative. But the truth of us is the balance of them all. Being right sized requires an admission of all our attributes. Since we are often required to deny or downplay our positive traits, indulgence is truth telling.

Spirit always responds to the truth. Thus, we experience our right size.

Indulgence - Journal

What attributes or reputations do I have that are pleasing to me? What do these say about me?

Not

Peter spoke to an older fellow, a spiritual elder. He explained the difficulties he experienced with the concept of God, beliefs he simply could not or would not embrace.

The elder replied very simply, "No question, if you've got problems with God, it's not God."

When Peter related this conversation, he added that the result of the elder's comment was instantaneous relief from his struggles; that it was never God with whom he battled, but his own conception of God.

There is a man who travels the country giving spiritual workshops. One of his most powerful techniques is to ask participants to write down what they believe about God. When he can get them to speak honestly, they often use such words as distant and demanding. He then asks who these negative attributes best fit, God or someone else. Invariably it is a parent or other caregiver, a minister or priest, or perhaps the student themselves.

The teacher then asks the participants to write down what they need from God. What follows is markedly different including ideas such as mercy, forgiveness, patience, compassion, and intimacy. At this the man gently suggests they ought to consider firing their old God, letting go of the old conception, and finding a new one that can give them what they need.

If you've got problems with God, it's not God.

Not - Journal

What problems do I have with God? What do I need? How might I go about finding a new God with whom I can do business?

_____

_____

_____

_____

_____

_____

_____

_____

_____

_____

_____

_____

Beyond

Old Bill had said it countless times. "I've got to get out of self. I've got to focus on others."

An older woman later responded, "It's more than focusing on others. I need to put myself in another person's shoes, to see and feel as they do. That's going beyond myself."

Still later, another elder added his thoughts. "The problem is I'm locked and loaded into my vantage point. I don't see *YOU*, I see you through *ME*." He laughed. "There's no question that God is going to have to solve that one for ME!" Others laughed with him freely.

Rhondell, creator of *The Science of Man*, spoke of objective awareness. He described it as a state beyond self, where even one's own self was viewed as an object. In other words, one no longer experiences through oneself because the self is no longer the point from which we perceive. He explained it was a state that could not be described, that it could only be experienced for oneself.

It may be useful to think in terms of my-self or our-selves, to consider that I am not "self," that self is only a package of conditioning. Then it may be helpful to consider how to view others from a framework other than of ME. Who are they, separate and apart from my perspective?

Getting out of self is certainly more complicated than we imagine.

Beyond - Journal

What are my current practices in getting out of self? What do I imagine it to be like to be beyond self?

_____

_____

_____

_____

_____

_____

_____

_____

_____

_____

_____

_____

_____

_____

115

Action

The congregation seemed almost to shift in response to a comment I made in the lesson. I had announced that any action would be less than effective if not preceded by contemplation. I even cited an authority for the statement, Father Richard Rohr, founder for the Center for Action and Contemplation.

Since the church had an activist nature, this was a troubling idea. Clearly some members believed that action was virtuous if the cause was virtuous. In fact, several members came to me after the service to challenge the idea. I did not retreat from my comments.

"Listen," I said to a passionate young woman. "We cannot know how things need to be, nor what ought to be done about them. That's true whether it's a person or culture we're confronting. So any action we take out of our sense of certainty is unlikely to be as effective as action that takes its direction from a Higher Source."

I could see I had provoked her. I took a deep breath and looked away for just a moment in order to listen for guidance. It came to me that I needed to apologize. Reluctantly, I inwardly released my argument while noticing her studying me.

"I'm sorry," I said. "It was not my goal to agitate you."

A look of surprise shot through her eyes. "You just did it, didn't you?"

I nodded as unexpected embarrassment flushed my face. I had been found out. I laughed, but did not reply.

She smiled before adding, "Cool!"

Action - Journal

When and how do I rush into action? What fuels me?

Gratitude

"Gratitude is an action, not a feeling," Patrick said.

I sat dumbfounded, lost in thought, completely bewildered by his comment.

"What good is any action if we have to feel good in order to take it?"

Now I was utterly confounded. Apparently it showed on my face, so Patrick gave me an assignment. "Every day do one good deed. But you can't do it because it feels good, but because it needs to be done. And you can't let anyone know about it."

I was baffled. I couldn't fathom such an idea.

Patrick laughed at my consternation. "Here's an example. Go into a public bathroom and pick up the toilet paper or paper towels on the floor. Better yet, do it when you're frustrated or annoyed, or when you don't want to." He winked at me before adding, "Don't tell anyone. It's gratitude in action."

For weeks I tried, and for weeks I failed, mostly because I couldn't keep from telling him the details.

Finally one day, I met the requirements and when I met with him announced in a self-satisfied voice, "I did a good deed, but I'm not going to tell you about it."

Immediately Patrick replied, "You just did ... it doesn't count."

At some point it all changed – gratitude in action – regardless of how I feel about it, and totally anonymous. I remain amazed at how difficult it can sometimes be.

Gratitude - Journal

Do a good deed today that you don't want to do and let no one know about it. How does it feel?

Controlled

"She was so upset that she cried when I told her," said my friend Bill.

If she is upset, she needs to be upset.

Lisa shook her head in bewilderment, "He just didn't get it. I was sad. It really frustrated him."

If he is frustrated, he needs to be frustrated.

"The guy was so annoyed he interrupted me right in the meeting. It was so inappropriate." Michele threw up her hands.

If they are annoyed, they need to be annoyed.

"Pissed me off, big time! I wanted to slug the bastard. Whack! Right up the side of his head." I caught the hint of a smile that flitted across my mouth as I described my reaction.

If I am angry, I need to be angry.

It seems crazy to take such an attitude as those described, far too tolerant. But that is culture speaking, and culture wants everyone and everything to be controlled. Culture wants to manage matters well. It is utterly impatient with upsets and troubles, seeking to deny and repress.

But what is … is. It matters not whether we like it, and it matters not whether we find it logical or rational. It is. They are. I am.

Controlled - Journal

How do I get upset, frustrated, annoyed or angered? Why is it that I might need these feelings and experiences?

_____

_____

_____

_____

_____

_____

_____

_____

_____

_____

_____

_____

_____

_____

_____

Exposed

My friend and rock climbing instructor reassured me, "It's fine and you're fine."

I replied, "Steve, you son-of-a-bitch, you didn't tell me, and now I can't go up or down."

We had climbed a very long chimney, protected on three sides. But the route took us onto exposed rock face six hundred feet above the valley below. While the crack onto which Steve was attempting to coax me was what he called a "bomber ledge," the loss of a feeling of security was overwhelming. With shaking legs and sweating palms, I wanted to cry, but got angry instead.

"You couldn't fall off of this if you wanted to," Steve urged me gently.

Of course, he was right. The danger was only an illusion, but that in no way diminished my fear. I now understood the notion of exposure, which is beyond rational thought.

Steve coaxed me along, and I did it.

This memory came back to me recently as I stood to speak before an audience. I was again feeling exposed. As I thought about it, I realized I have spent much of my life feeling exposed and afraid.

I remembered that in the realm of Spirit, there is nothing to fear.

Open yourself up. Raise your chin. Throw back your shoulders. Expose your throat and your heart to people and the world. Dare to risk. There is nothing to fear and nothing to flee.

We can't fail, even if we wanted to.

Exposed - Journal

Where do I feel exposed in my life? What exactly are the feelings, and where do I hold them in my body?

_____

_____

_____

_____

_____

_____

_____

_____

_____

_____

_____

_____

_____

_____

_____

Anima

They call it flat affect. Julie's voice was somewhat monotone, and her facial features were constrained. There was little in the way of obvious emotion. No anima - Spirit was obviously obscured.

I wondered about Julie's life story. Few children are born without natural animation. Something had happened to stifle her: trauma or tragedy. Somewhere beneath her featurelessness, Spirit stirred.

It was a dramatic contrast to only hours before when I ate lunch with another woman, Karen. She had been bursting with anima, Spirit seemingly unable to find enough room to express fully. She had lively green eyes that followed every movement around her, and her face was readily swept by feelings that registered fully. She laughed a lot, and her body literally danced with movement.

The body is no more than a container, a skin-covered residence for Spirit. Infinity indwells us.

Imagine children. They dance and sing and laugh. They yell and cry and have tantrums. Sitting still can be very difficult. Curiosity abounds. Spirit is in motion, endlessly expressing.

Still we seek to contain the infinite, to hold expression within socially acceptable bounds. We attempt to stifle anima ... Spirit, though we ultimately fail. For every aspect of us that is contained, another will emerge, even if only in our imagination or dreams.

Spirit soars, and so must we.

Anima - Journal

How do I try to contain myself? How do I try to get others to contain themselves? What are my motives?

_____

_____

_____

_____

_____

_____

_____

_____

_____

_____

_____

_____

_____

125

Fixed

Dave was adamant. I smiled at him in the midst of the conversation. "You're going to hold onto that heavy metal identify no matter what, aren't you?" I asked.

In response, a mischievous light twinkled in his eyes and a grin spread across his lips. He neither confirmed nor denied my observation, but the answer was obvious.

We chatted about his old idea for a while. Dave believed with certainty that life was a brutal struggle, that it was the grim battle which gave life meaning. His telling response to any other possibility was a sarcastic one, "I'm not going to do all that rainbows, daisies, and unicorns crap."

He was beautiful in his defiance, and it reminded me of a moment of my own. One day with a therapist, I inadvertently bumped into a deeply held belief, one fixed in my psyche. We discovered it when I said, "Love means giving yourself up."

The therapist responded, "Really?"

In an instant I raged within. I wanted to hit the therapist. Then I wanted to flee. His innocent question brought my fixed belief into the light, and a short while later I was crying as I released an old idea that no longer served me well.

As Dave and I parted I asked a seemingly innocent question. "Do you suppose your heavy metal belief serves you any longer?"

Dave flinched a bit. I grinned at him then added, "Who said you had to suffer? And who said God was the cause?"

Fixed - Journal

What old ideas or fixed beliefs do I insist upon? What would it take to call them into question?

_____

_____

_____

_____

_____

_____

_____

_____

_____

_____

_____

_____

_____

Persistence

As usual, I was right on time. Every six weeks or so, I experienced an emotional upheaval that might range from disappointment to full-blown meltdown. While the subjects were invariably different, the timing was very predictable.

Over several years a host of people coaxed me through these challenging times. Eventually my emotions moderated, but the pattern remained intact.

A recurring spiritual message is the importance of persistence. In fact, I have been told that the proper translation of an often cited Christian scripture is in fact, "Keep knocking. Keep seeking. Keep asking." This idea reminds me of the phrase from the tumultuous 1960s, "Keep on keeping on."

My emotional responses are the inevitable and natural consequence of persistence. Regardless of how much freedom I may gain from self-will, to be human is to have will and to attempt to exercise it. Predictably, with each new effort comes frustration as well as the assurance that progress will result.

The best-selling book *The Greatest Salesman in the World* offers as one of its tenets, "I will persist until I succeed."

Persistence is holy ground, a gift from The Divine that leads us toward awareness, if we can only practice it.

Persistence - Journal

How would I characterize my ability to persist? What frustration emerges as a result? What progress can I see?

Small

Molly played small. It may have been an infantile survival tactic, but it fit with the part of her that was still an infant despite her actual age of twenty-eight.

Molly's story was a fairly common one. Her father had been domineering and hypercritical of her as long as she could remember. Nothing she had ever done was adequate. And his voice had taken full-time, rent-free residence in her mind. Her father's abusive comments had become her own.

Her conditioning had likely been established very early in life, though it had adapted over time to be more socially workable. Still, you could see it in her posture: shoulders rolled slightly forward in self-defense and a slight downward and deferent angle to her chin. The accounts of her life were filled with self-condemnation and strategies to minimize her exposure to criticism. In total, they were a strategy of smallness in response to a terrifying foe.

There came a day when Molly was able for the first time to shake off her fears. It was initially very brief, but grew over several years until the day came when she threw back her shoulders and exposed herself to the world.

In that moment a glorious Molly emerged. She was fully herself, and the possibilities terrified her. She shrank again, but only for a while. She could no longer deny herself.

So it is with all of us. Smallness gives way to our own wondrous reality. Spirit shines forth, and we are finally home and whole.

Small – Journal

How do I play small?

_____

_____

_____

_____

_____

_____

_____

_____

_____

_____

_____

_____

_____

_____

_____

Greatness

Tears creep into my eyes as I consider the tale of my greatest achievement. It came as my second wife and I worked out the terms of our divorce. Natalie and Brianne, my stepdaughters, wanted to know how my split from their mom would affect them.

I told the girls, my daughters, that I had come to love them and that I had made commitments to them. The fact that their mother and I were splitting had no bearing. Nothing would change.

There was skepticism in their eyes, though they appreciated my reassurance. What they did not know was that I had had many discussions with trusted friends on this matter. I had concluded that love was a principle, and demonstration was its proof.

Five years have passed and my actions have exceeded my highest expectations. As a result, I have two daughters who love me very much. I can describe any number of occasions where I have fallen short in so many ways in my life. But in this one instance, I am fortunate to have risen to a level I never dreamed possible.

I am profoundly humbled by the telling of my experience of greatness. It is greatness for which Spirit's credit must be acknowledged.

But it is mine to relish.

Greatness - Journal

What is my moment of greatness? What or who made it possible? How does it make me feel?

_____

_____

_____

_____

_____

_____

_____

_____

_____

_____

_____

_____

_____

Benign

Andrea said, "It's not like I can grow a new leg. And God doesn't bring back someone who has died. So how can you say that anything can be made right?"

The teacher smiled and nodded his head. "Of course such healings are not typical. But first, be assured they have occurred. So do not discount them out of hand."

The teacher cocked his head to study Andrea. After a few moments of listening he nodded again in assurance before proceeding.

"We have no way of knowing what it means to have something made right. But we do know that such rightness will be accompanied by inner peace. Often the circumstance can best be compared to a malignant tumor that is killing the body. We need not necessarily rid the body of the tumor, but render it benign."

He paused again.

"For example Andrea, let's take the pain you feel for your son. He was killed accidentally, yet you remain wounded nearly a decade later. Still you cannot consider having another child because of your pain and fear. Yes?"

Andrea somberly agreed.

"Good. The point is that you have a malignancy that is killing you. We cannot change the death. But through our efforts, we can change your current experience of it. The facts will remain, but their poison will be gone. They will become benign."

The teacher smiled broadly. "That would make it right wouldn't it?"

Benign - Journal

Choosing some area of unresolved pain or fear in my life, what would it take to have it made right?

Radiating

Children darted around the playground, laughing and chattering incessantly. At the far end of the schoolyard, a group of young men battled aggressively on the basketball court, sweating and cursing. A contingent of slender, adolescent women talked as they watched, occasionally giggling at the sometimes wild actions of the men. Around the perimeter of the grass an old man and woman walked slowly but steadily as a mother jogging behind a high-tech stroller swiftly passed them. Auras haloed around each body, fading into the background energy of earth and sky, grass and brick.

There's an old Jewish story of men gambling and carousing while a rabbi does nothing but smile knowingly at their antics. Even as their conduct escalates far beyond the proscribed rules of their religion, the rabbi patiently observes. A concerned member of the community asks the spiritual leader why he does not intervene.

He replies with great gentleness and understanding, "When their zeal turns to God, it will be glorious to see."

Said a wise man from a backwater town in rural Texas, "We cannot not be God's kids."

Around the schoolyard, the children of Spirit are laughing, cursing, chatting, walking and running. They ooze holiness in all that they are and do. What we are speaks so loudly, it matters not what we do. The challenge is to see Spirit radiating forth in every imaginable expression.

Radiating - Journal

What actions or inactions of others are the hardest for me to see Spirit within? Why?

_____

_____

_____

_____

_____

_____

_____

_____

_____

_____

_____

_____

Expanding

Lefty said it in the middle of the gathering, and it was obvious it immediately changed the course for many of those participating. He said, "For years, every time I thought I'd arrived, I later found it was just one more plateau in my growth. Each plateau eventually revealed another emotional, psychological or spiritual elevation ahead. It doesn't ever seem to end."

The group's conversation shifted. Suddenly everyone sounded like travelers rather than those who had arrived.

A few minutes later, Bebop offered an arresting question, "So who's in charge of this spiritual journey?"

The silence was deafening. Apparently, everyone simultaneously realized that all their personal observations and experiences were dwarfed by the magnitude of the implication. Egos suddenly shrunk.

Tim then added very quietly, "Not me."

Laughter rippled through the men as Jeffrey spoke. "It's big, and getting bigger all the time."

Lefty spoke again. He asked, "Can you feel it getting bigger right now?"

Silence again fell on the group.

Always a larger container for knowing. Always more to experience. Always deeper connection available. Always expanding. Never ending.

Expanding - Journal

How large is my spiritual container? Can I see it growing?
Does it expand to be filled, or does filling create expansion?

_____

_____

_____

_____

_____

_____

_____

_____

_____

_____

_____

_____

_____

Manna

There is a biblical story of the Jews wandering in the wilderness for a very long time. Each day the unleavened bread known as manna fell from heaven to be collected as dew from the leaves of plants. At the end of the day, the manna was no more, it had no life beyond the day of its fall. It seems the Jews were required to live not just in the day's sustenance, but in trust the needs of the next day would be met as well.

In a more modern setting, a spiritual advisor delivered the same message. In fact, he said it several ways, but one seemed most accurate. "Yesterday's contact with Spirit is insufficient for today. It must be made new each day."

So each day we begin anew. That which we understood, or knew, or experienced at some past date is of no use to us today unless it produces new spiritual fruitage.

Once there was a man who had no belief in God. It was not that he opposed the idea of the Divine, only that he knew nothing of it.

A friend of the man was always puzzled by the man's actions, for each day the man would pray and meditate. The friend asked him, "Aren't you a hypocrite? You do not believe in God and yet you pray?"

The man laughed. "It works. I don't know why, and I don't know how. But it works. So each day I try to be quiet and I try to pray."

Manna - Journal

Can I identify the manna in my life? What practices do I engage in so that it may be received?

_____

_____

_____

_____

_____

_____

_____

_____

_____

_____

_____

_____

Death

On a number of occasions I have chatted with people experiencing the death of some aspect of themselves, the diminishment of attributes attached to their ego. In each case, there has been discomfort. Yet each time a quiet resolve has dominated, ultimately replacing or overlaying their uneasiness.

Some years ago, as a hospice volunteer, I watched patients as death approached. While decency kept me from inquiring into their dying experience, their comments suggested the same kind of quiet resolve eventually came to many of them.

It seems that in facing the demise of the ego, a greater force takes hold. Acceptance is its sign, accompanied by certainty and calm that are demonstrations of Spirit's presence.

Yet the appearance of acceptance is mysterious. There are few people or occasions where acceptance can be produced by will or choice. Instead it arrives on quiet wings unannounced, emerging from the battle that precedes it.

My teacher calls that battle the machine. It must run its course. When resistance is finished, acceptance magically appears with its attendant peace.

"I'm just tired of fighting it," said one acquaintance struggling with core character challenges. "So I'm prepared to face it."

Interestingly, it is acceptance that provided the entrance for Spirit and for healing.

Perhaps we would benefit from accepting the process of death as well as the resistance that ultimately yields peace … to cease fighting and abandon the fight itself.

Death - Journal

To what do I continue to cling? How does this further my ultimate acceptance?

Supply

We had just finished listening to a recording of the teachings of a spiritual master. In it, as a demonstration of supply, he described the experience of Captain Eddie Rickenbacher. The captain and his crew were lost at sea for three weeks during the dry season. Nonetheless, daily rains provided drinking water. Food appeared with fish literally jumping into the boat and birds landing on Rickenbacher's head.

I commented that I wished I could experience such spiritual demonstration. Louis looked at me quizzically. "Ron?" he said in an exaggerated voice.

"What?" I replied with equal exaggeration.

With exasperation and more volume Louis again said, "Ron?"

I blinked my eyes a few times as I contemplated his reaction. Then it registered. I grinned at him sheepishly.

"Oh!" I replied. "You mean I've already got it, don't you?"

Louis grinned back at me.

As usual I simply couldn't see the truth. For more than ten years, consulting and speaking opportunities have been appearing out of nowhere. For more than twenty years, cash flow has manifested sufficiently and sometimes mysteriously, always providing.

I shook my head as Louis cocked his head knowingly.

"Okay. I see. But just once I'd like a bird to land on my head so I could remember that supply is ever present. What's wrong with a little miracle?"

Lewis again looked at me strangely and with still greater exasperation announced, "RON!"

Supply - Journal

Where is the evidence of supply in my life? What are the impediments to recognizing it?

Believe

If we want to know what we believe, look at what we do. That is evidence of our belief.

This is the story of my struggles to learn to believe. I've always professed belief in God, though what I believe about that God has changed. Yet what has been constant are the actions which suggest I do not believe.

I heard it asked once, "If so many profess a belief in heaven, a place that is to be heavenly, why is there such fear of death?"

Ron, if you believe in a Spirit that can be trusted to handle the affairs and outcomes of your life, why are you so insistently self-reliant? If you believe this Spirit is perfectly present and perfectly responsive to your needs, why are you so willful? If you believe It will provide, why have you worried so much about sufficient income and means?

These are disturbing questions, revealing a notable gap between what I profess and what I apparently believe. Proof is in the action.

When troubles arise, Ron, do you turn to prayer and the Divine or leap into action? When uncertainly lies before you, do you trustingly relax and allow the movement of Spirit or do you concoct plans layered upon plans? What is it you fear?

There is no obvious reason for my fears, I am simply afraid. And the solution lies within me.

But experience has slowly weaned me from some of my self-reliance. A body of belief has grown based on evidence. It now permits a degree of belief I once could not muster.

The important thing is to see the truth of what I do and do not believe.

Believe - Journal

What do I profess to believe? What does my behavior suggest are my actual beliefs?

_____

_____

_____

_____

_____

_____

_____

_____

_____

_____

_____

_____

_____

Watching

There's a little boy in a stroller at the zoo. His parents have taken him to see many of the sights, animatedly pointing toward the giraffes, and later the seals and sea lions. They are very excited about showing him the animals.

The boy quietly watches, noticing not only the beasts and birds, but the actions and antics of his mother and father. He sucks thoughtfully on a juice box, obviously studying everything that crosses his line of sight. At one moment he gazes upward into massive trees, at another he watches a paper wrapper spinning madly in a small dervish of wind.

There is much to see in the foreground, or the object of his focus. Yet there is infinitely more to see in the background. The boy simply watches, perhaps without opinion. That would explain his quiet contemplation.

What does the boy see? Colors? Shapes? Movement? His parents provide the interpretation as well as a steady stream of their emotion. At what moment does watching cease and knowing begin? When does he come to fear the big cats and venomous snakes? In the instant he comes to love a particular creature, what is the source of his feeling?

There is a watcher at work in the little boy, a watcher that will be lulled into knowingness at some point. For now, he sees paradise. At some future date, the watcher may reawaken; or it may remain dormant his entire life. He may find freedom, or he may not.

For now, he is watching and seeing.

Watching - Journal

I take a moment now and watch my surroundings? What do I see? What is my interpretation? What is real?

_____

_____

_____

_____

_____

_____

_____

_____

_____

_____

_____

_____

_____

Nothing

The group became edgy as soon as it was said. "I need do nothing. Relax and take it easy."

Immediately a man's hand shot up. He said urgently, "But of course we must take action. Right?"

The teacher simply shook his head. "I need do nothing."

The statement struck the man in an almost physical way. He recoiled from the words and might have spoken again if another had not leapt into the fray.

"That's crazy! God helps those who help themselves!"

Now the teacher grinned. "I need do nothing for there is nothing to be done."

With this, the group suddenly became quiet. A woman with light in her eyes quietly asked, "Things aren't what we think, are they?"

The teacher's smile grew larger. "God alone is initiative. We need do nothing."

Collectively, a feeling almost like a big sigh swept through the room. Truth relaxed them, almost as one.

We need do nothing. Relax and take it easy. We are in good hands, hands that have held us all along. There is nothing that needs to be done.

Nothing – Journal

Just for this moment, consider doing nothing. Contemplate that nothing needs doing. What do I feel in response?

Validation

It was a training session in public speaking, and the group gathered was providing feedback to one of its participants. The feedback was extensive and predominantly critical. As each comment came, the woman upon whom they were focused seemed to shrink just a little further into herself. At one point, one of the evaluators said he was sorry to be so harsh, but that it was for her own good.

My opportunity came. I complimented her on her smile, her posture and her authenticity. I told her it was the latter trait that won me over, that who she was simply rang out in her presentation. "Well done," I concluded.

She beamed at me. She was restored.

It has been said that for every single criticism we level at a child, it will take sixteen acts of praise to counteract it. I think it is not much different with adults, though we've been hardened over the years and don't readily show our hurt.

There is an argument that says we must provide critique, else people cannot know how to improve. There is a counter argument that says it is validation we need, that we are inherent learners and only need encouragement.

This much I know. Each time I genuinely compliment or praise, the recipient is validated. When I learn authentic appreciation of others, I can even critique without injury because it is offered in a validating fashion.

In the end, each of us seems to want nothing more than to know we are valued. Validation is the key, and authenticity it's currency. Literally, we see their spiritual being, and in response they feel seen.

Validation - Journal

Who have I validated recently? Who have I critiqued? In each case, how was it offered to them? In the end, did they feel valued?

_____

_____

_____

_____

_____

_____

_____

_____

_____

_____

_____

_____

_____

Failure

It was a typical professional setting and audience. I stood before the leaders projecting calm, confidence, and success. Little did they know what I had in store for them.

For ninety minutes we interacted about a wide range of leadership concerns. On several occasions I introduced spiritual concepts, and each was well received, even though they were not traditional leadership concepts.

As the end of the seminar approached, I returned again to my initial theme. "Seeing True is that moment when we fully comprehend the truth of some matter, situation, or person." I paused before adding, "It changes everything when we see it."

I felt anxiety rise in my chest as I approached the moment of revelation. "Let me tell you that you have misperceived me all night. I am not who you think I am. You have been misled by my appearance, my words and my reputation. But you need to know the truth in order to see me true, and thus to see you true."

It was very, very quiet in the room. I had their undivided attention.

"Twenty years ago, I was thrown out of my profession. My wife left me. I experienced serious mental health issues and several severe health problems. And I discovered I was alcoholic."

I shook my head. "You need to know these facts about me. Otherwise, you will leave here thinking you are not like me. And you will not see that failure made me, and that you are not alone in your adversities. Failure is not as it seems, and neither are we."

Failure - Journal

What are my failures? How might they be assets?

One

It is said that the third time is a charm, and so it seemed.

The day had begun with a conversation with a friend, Art. Chatting about a budding relationship in my life, I observed I was quite tickled as well as puzzled with how he and I were able to talk so well with each other.

Art quickly spoke, "Of course. God's just enjoying talking to God. It's Oneness."

In all honesty, his comment didn't quite register until later in the day. Neither did a comment I offered later in a conversation with a young woman who had just asked me to work with her on some challenging inner demons. I found myself saying, "You're imbued with Spirit. It's all One."

In fact, it didn't add up until that evening as I sat on a lawn after a fine dinner with two friends involved in a spiritual activity, Laurie and Stephen. Laurie wondered about the meaning of *The Course in Miracles*, and we had been chatting about her question as well as the notion of atonement ... at-one-ment.

Just before we said goodbye, Stephen observed, "You know, there is only one miracle. It should be *The Course in Miracle*."

We laughed easily.

And then it finally registered. Three times I'd heard the message that day.

One. Not two of anything. One.

One - Journal

What are those places and circumstances that reveal Oneness to me?

_____

_____

_____

_____

_____

_____

_____

_____

_____

_____

_____

_____

_____

Relating

"Did you get it?" I asked the six workshop participants.

They stared at me blankly.

"Let me repeat it then. Relationship is fiction. Relating is holy ground."

This time a young woman, Eve, nodded in agreement. And I nodded to encourage her to share.

She spoke tentatively. "Since there is only God, then God in me relates to God in you. That's relating." She eyed me cautiously to see if she was on track. I smiled and again nodded.

"So relating is active ... in the now. Relationship is a human attempt to freeze God. That kills the Spirit in relating, renders it false, a fiction."

Two more heads nodded.

I prodded her further. "So what are we to do, Eve?"

I watched as she listened for inner guidance. I could almost see the invisible strand connecting Spirit in her to Spirit around her.

She took a breath and focused back on the setting around her. Then she giggled, though she tried mightily not to. But it overtook her and she burst out in gales of laughter. Soon her companions were laughing with her, though they didn't know why.

Long moments passed before she was able to compose herself. She took a measured breath to center herself.

"Sorry," Eve said with a grin from ear to ear, "Spirit wanted to laugh."

"And," I asked. "What are we to do?"

She announced, "Try not to screw it up." She snorted, unable to contain her merriment, and collapsed into howls of laughter.

Relating - Journal

If relating is Spirit in me interacting with Spirit in others, what are the ways that I try to turn it into relationship?

_____

_____

_____

_____

_____

_____

_____

_____

_____

_____

_____

_____

_____

_____

Unconditional

The party swirled around us as we connected in intimate conversation. Hal and Camille had recently heard me give a speech at a church and were asking for clarification on some remarks I had made about Divine love.

I was puzzled because I could not recall saying what they heard. I related a funny story about a woman coming up to me some years ago and thanking me for saving her life. She proceeded to describe something I had said, and I was virtually certain I could never have said such a thing.

It was my first mentor who told me that my best work would be done when I was not aware of it; and my current mentor has often noted that when Spirit has full access to express as me, words will simply fall from my mouth and I will know it is not me speaking. In words captured from the New Testament, "Christ liveth my life."

A burst of raucous laughter yanked me back to the party and Hal and Camille. I admitted I could not recall my comments about Divine love. Then I paused and used a technique taught to me by a wise woman. I quietly listened for what wanted to be said, took a deep breath, opened my mouth and spoke.

"We're told God is love. But we confuse it with a rich and tempting rush of emotions. That's not it. God's love has two attributes. The first is that it is without condition. Carl Rogers called it unconditional positive regard. There is nothing we can do to earn it, nor to forfeit it. And it is utterly without judgment. The second attribute is that it is available unceasingly. It is always present and never withheld. Our experiences are its perfect expression."

I shrugged sheepishly and laughed. Hal and Camille laughed with me.

Unconditional - Journal

If Divine love is unconditional, without judgment and ever present, how is it demonstrated through me today?

_____

_____

_____

_____

_____

_____

_____

_____

_____

_____

_____

_____

_____

Present

During a trip to several Indian reservations in Arizona, our guides did an admirable job of illustrating and explaining the cultures and their differences. After a childhood spent enamored of American Indians and reading every book on them in our town library, I was enthralled with everything I was shown and told.

But of all the information I received during that tour, I was dumbfounded by the explanation that some of the ancient languages had nothing but a present tense, no past or future. At first blush I was puzzled, but subsequent explanation left me awed.

There is the present moment. And there is the present moment that occurred yesterday. And there is a present moment that will occur tomorrow. All exists in the present, thus there is no need for past or future tense because in fact there is no past or future, only the present.

I remember seeing the wisdom of that perspective, the certainty that every spoken utterance was a confirmation of the present.

From this awareness came a still small voice whispering to me. *I am only in the present moment. There is no God of past or future, only of this instant.*

It took my breath away and I understood why being in the present is so powerful. The past and future are fiction, and Truth is in the present. Being in Truth is the only Truth.

Present - Journal

Breathe. Breath is in the present. Breathe. Breath is here and now. Breathe. What do I feel?

_____

_____

_____

_____

_____

_____

_____

_____

_____

_____

_____

_____

_____

_____

Innocent

I was facilitating a workshop on leadership at a convention when we began to examine our assumptions about people. Many opinions were expressed based on unconscious misunderstandings. A thought arose that I promptly ignored. But it recurred several times, and I was afraid to broach the subject with the group. This was a very conservative crowd and would be quite resistant to the idea. But as the misunderstandings continued among them, I finally took a deep breath and spoke.

"If we are to lead people, or even get along with them, we must understand they are not bad, dumb or evil." I braced myself. "Those guys who flew airplanes into the World Trade Center believed they were living their highest expression through their actions."

It was very quiet in the room. "Not one of us does anything that we think is wrong at that moment. We may be deluded. We may be ignorant. We may be naive. But rest assured none of our actions are inherently evil."

The stillness deepened; I relaxed into it as I waited. After a few long moments I felt the next words emerge.

"We don't have to like it. But if we are to rise to our full potential, we have to find a way to look at everyone and say, even if only to ourselves, 'You're innocent.'"

A woman raised her hand and asked, "Are you telling me I must see my drug-addicted daughter as innocent?"

The response came instantly. "Yes. I would tell her, 'You're innocent, and I love you. You're innocent, and I love you. You're innocent.'"

The only path is to see we're all innocent.

Innocent - Journal

Choosing someone or some action I find completely unacceptable, why am I unable to see innocence? What would it take to see otherwise?

_____

_____

_____

_____

_____

_____

_____

_____

_____

_____

_____

_____

_____

_____

Abandonment

A small community of spiritual seekers asked me to spend a day facilitating a workshop in personal transformation. They were long-term students of metaphysics who still sought to break through the difficulties of their lives. They remained stuck despite their studies and efforts.

On a number of occasions, I noticed they spoke of personal surrender, a need to give something up. In the middle of the afternoon, words poured from me that I had not planned and could not have predicted.

"The mischief in your approach is in the idea of surrender. I have no evidence from any of my work that anyone ever gives up something they still value. I see no proof of what you call surrender. Not with you. Not with me. Not with anyone."

The room became very still and I could almost hear egos cracking open.

"Spirit will take nothing from us, if we still desire it. So the issue is in no longer valuing something."

The shift was beginning. It was apparent in their eyes.

"Abandonment is what we seek. We need to abandon the manifestations of self, and in order for us to abandon anything, it must lose its value, either because we see it cannot provide what we seek, or because we find something of greater value."

One of the women gasped in surprise. "It's going to hurt to no longer want to control," she stated with tears welling in her eyes. "But it doesn't work."

Nodding gently toward her as another woman touched her, I concurred. "That's the prayer. It doesn't work and I don't want it. Then Spirit can act."

Abandonment - Journal

What things do I still value that in truth I ought to examine?
What still hurts me? What prevents me from growing? What must I
abandon?

_____

_____

_____

_____

_____

_____

_____

_____

_____

_____

_____

_____

_____

Truth

Mahatma Gandhi said, "I am committed to truth, not consistency. To which one of my friends said, "What the hell does that mean?"

In order to have a glimpse into Gandhi's perspective, we must borrow from the words of Joel Goldsmith. "If you can touch, taste or smell it, or even describe it, rest assured it is not It." As a result, Goldsmith arrived at the term Infinite Invisible.

At any moment, the most we can perceive of the Divine is nothing more than a facet of the whole. Thus our understanding and our beliefs at any given moment are based only in a small piece of Truth. To stand fast on that single perspective is to insist upon an absolute which is, in fact, not absolute.

While consistency may be comfortable and comforting, it is at best shortsighted and at worst close-minded.

Committing to Truth is to be open to more being revealed. It is to affirm that we can know only a little. More importantly, it is to be willing to release our certainties and our beliefs on a moment's notice, to risk not just how we appear to others but also our own sense of knowingness. It is to live in an insecurity of self, trusting there is larger security beyond self.

What then is Truth?

Perhaps it is so vast that we cannot conceive of it. Perhaps it is that which is left when all our senses, conceptions and beliefs of it are cast aside.

Truth - Journal

What senses, conceptions, and beliefs of the Divine do I still cling to?

Connection

Connection is our only purpose.

When this idea is offered up for consideration, it will typically cause a pause in thought and action. Then the crescendo of debate begins.

But what about loving and being loved? How about the pursuit of happiness, preferably mine? Or the acquisition of belongings that will bring me pleasure and comfort? What of the drive toward self-actualization?

Connection is our only purpose, and the only state that will bring the satisfaction, fulfillment and contentment we seek.

When we are in "the zone" we are fully connected. This is a state of being fully in the moment and the activities of the moment.

Beyond this is a realm of conscious connection, a heightened state of awareness, or Oneness. At its highest expression, there is no separation between Creator and created. Awareness gives way to Communion, which then yields to Union. One.

Whether connection is conscious or unconscious is not our concern, though the drive to increase conscious contact will serve us well.

When we come to experience great connection, everything else is added. It may come as finances or companionship, opportunities or success. While these will be appropriate to our circumstances, we will no longer seek them.

Connection is our only purpose.

Connection - Journal

To what am I attached? What do I pursue in seeking my fulfillment? If these are not connection, how might I seek otherwise?

_____

_____

_____

_____

_____

_____

_____

_____

_____

_____

_____

_____

_____

Adorable

Alicia lit up as she described her experience. For no apparent reason, she found herself feeling adorable for nearly a day and a half. It was not an emotional state with which she was familiar, but she enjoyed it thoroughly. After recounting it, she beamed.

Then she explained how she made no attempt to hold onto the state or recover it when the experience waned. Intuitively, Alicia knew she had received a gift that she could not claim. It was to be enjoyed and appreciated, which proved to be an easy task.

Initially, Alicia had been hesitant to describe her experience. On one hand, she thought it might seem too strange. On the other, there was a certain embarrassment in admitting she had been feeling adorable. Both reactions were hardly surprising. There is nothing in our cultural underpinnings to encourage feeling whole or speaking of it.

Yet we are all adorable. While few have the opportunity to feel it, denying it once we have experienced it is to immerse ourselves in reverse pride.

Ultimately, adorable is our natural state. Knowing it for ourselves is a mighty step. Coming to see it in everyone we encounter is greater still.

The look on Alicia's face said it all. In experiencing adorable, she became adorable.

Adorable - Journal

In what ways am I able to appreciate myself? How do I feel it? How do I express it? Can I see it in others?

_____

_____

_____

_____

_____

_____

_____

_____

_____

_____

_____

_____

_____

Selfish

Two friends joined me for breakfast and conversation. I challenged them with a question I had heard recently while traveling in Texas.

"So ... you're opening the door for someone. It's a thoughtful gesture. Are you doing it for them? Or are you doing it to please yourself? Or for that matter, are you doing it to gain their approval?"

Both men paused, sensing a trap.

Then Jeff announced, "Let me step right into this and screw it up." He chuckled. "If I don't get anything out of it, why do it?"

His comment caused us all to laugh.

The late Anthony de Mello, a Jesuit priest who was removed from his order, had it right. We can choose to please ourselves by doing that which pleases us. Or we can choose to please ourselves by pleasing others. Regardless, we're still selfish.

This is a daunting matter to consider. Is there not a higher motivation?

Therein lies a powerful secret. A higher intention is one of enlightened self-interest. It recognizes that self-centeredness is central to being human. First, we must tell this truth to ourselves, that we are selfish and self-centered.

A greater calling is not possible without first admitting this reality.

Then we seek to bring ourselves into alignment with a greater purpose or Higher Power. It is this alignment that makes all things possible.

Selfish - Journal

In what ways am I selfish? Do I please myself by pleasing me or pleasing others? Is there inner resistance to this idea?

_____

_____

_____

_____

_____

_____

_____

_____

_____

_____

_____

_____

_____

Forgiveness

"Rest assured," Sam said, "If you believe you've been done wrong, you'll retaliate."

"I can see that," I replied. "So the secret to forgiveness is in not experiencing a wrong." I paused then continued, "Regardless of what the other person does."

Sam nodded, and I quickly recounted a recent conversation with a man who had asked me for guidance. Daniel had said to me as he arrived at the coffee shop for our meeting, "Sorry I'm late, some son of a bitch cut me off in traffic and I clipped someone else. Nothing major, but man am I pissed."

"Ah," I responded in a wise tone. "So the guy cut YOU off. "

Daniel promptly agreed, overlooking my emphasis.

I continued. "So the guy looked over his shoulder, saw you, and said, 'There's that guy Daniel who I'm going to cut off, cause to have an accident, and really piss off.' Or was there some other way he selected you out?"

A look of annoyance passed over Daniel's face. An instant later he laughed. "Okay, what's the point?"

"The point is that we presume wrong being done to us, and therein lies the misperception. Let go of the idea that anyone ever intends such a thing, and you'll discover a secret to forgiveness."

Daniel stared at me wordlessly.

I smiled at him. "Yep, there ain't no wrong to be righted. That's what it means to forgive."

Forgiveness - Journal

What wrongs do I perceive? How do I retaliate in response to those wrongs?

_____

_____

_____

_____

_____

_____

_____

_____

_____

_____

_____

_____

Party

Modern culture has deep and profound beliefs about individual rights. America exemplifies this with freedom of speech, civil rights, and even the right to the pursuit of happiness.

Yet all these can be taken from us, if not by legal means, then by illness or death. So if they can be taken away, are they then rights?

Consider the possibility that in truth we are granted many privileges. Perhaps it is good fortune to be given life. And maybe everything that comes into that life, whether person, situation or thing, is in fact a gift.

Why a gift? If not a gift, then we must somehow prove how we've earned it. Since we can take no credit for our life, aptitudes or skills, then we must consider anything received as coming from beyond ourselves, our thoughts, or our actions. For who among us can create a being, bring a thought into existence, or perform an action?

Oh, but we do believe we can think and act. The proof of this misunderstanding is easily demonstrated. Try to describe and replicate the exact neuromuscular phenomena that allow one to read a single word on this page.

It may be that we are invited guests at the party of life. It may be that there is no charge and no requirement.

Perhaps our only right lies in the opportunity to awaken and thereby fully experience the party, the guests, and our incredibly good fortune.

Party - Journal

What do I insist are rights for me? For others? Who told me they are rights? What proof do I have?

_____

_____

_____

_____

_____

_____

_____

_____

_____

_____

_____

_____

_____

Ecstasy

I'm watching the movie, "Spiderman," on television, hardly the expected time and place for a spiritual experience. I feel a lightness in my chest that increases over the next half hour until the end of the movie. I notice it, but am still not really aware that something is afoot.

It's only when I lay on the bed to read before going to sleep that distractions fall away and I am suddenly overwhelmed with feeling. It is overpowering in its intensity, and my entire body is quickly pulsing with it.

I breathe into the now enormous fullness of my heart, and my body begins to writhe in ecstasy. It's almost more than I can stand, and my mind tries to slip away over and over again to something else. But I stay with my breath and the feelings, which are indescribably pleasant, like a non-sexual, whole body orgasm.

Gratitude fills me, and I weep as my body continues contorting in pleasure. Self-consciousness finally drops away and I am able to simply experience the Divine visitation.

More than an hour passes before I am released. I am spent.

A memory comes to me. That morning I had renounced several aspects of self. Simultaneously, as I asked to be relieved of them, I humbly requested to be taken to a new level on my path. Perfect response to a prayer that was unusually honest for me. I wanted more than anything to feel Spirit. Ecstasy was the answer.

It is said that one cannot describe nor understand Spirit, that the only authentic knowing is experiential.

I don't know.

Ecstasy - Journal

When have I experienced the Sacred? What were the conditions that set the scene for the experience?

_____

_____

_____

_____

_____

_____

_____

_____

_____

_____

_____

_____

_____

Index

Afterword

One of the great gifts of *Seeing True* is compassion for ourselves and for others. In my experience, it is learned through the often painful and always disquieting human foibles that so frequently appear in us. Of late, I have taken to calling them the squalls of my humanity. Into the midst of a perfectly tranquil and orderly moment, a burst of selfness suddenly appears. The next thing I know, I've said or done something foolish or inconsiderate. As a result, I feel discomfort, guilt or shame.

In my journey and in my work with others, I have discovered that many of us have little tolerance or patience for shortcomings in ourselves or others. In *Seeing True,* a possibility arises to cease judging and condemning. In that potential are the seeds of forgiveness and compassion. In the end, these lead to the realization of innocence - for everyone.

If we were to know all, we would see there is nothing to forgive. Everything is perfectly manifest, and each of us is innocent. We always have been and always will be, regardless of our human tendencies. We are innocent. That is *Seeing True.*

Hummingbirds

Many of my materials feature hummingbirds. I find them beautiful, but there's another reason for their use.

In addition to being a symbol of joy in some indigenous cultures, the tale of the hummingbird is extraordinary.

Migrating up to 6,000 miles from South America to the American Southwest while losing half its already minimal weight of one ounce, a hummingbird can return to the same backyard each year. Failing to find the expected feeder and assuming human negligence, they are known to rap on windows to announce their arrival.

I have named my company Magnetic North, LLC, as a tribute to this remarkable capacity in hummingbirds. It is by magnetic north that these extraordinary creatures orient themselves.

Each of us has our own magnetic north that will guide us as unerringly as the hummingbird. Discover it ... learn to navigate by it ... and it will transform your life.

In the meantime, enjoy the journey.

Author's Page

Ronald Chapman has followed many paths of spiritual and religious study over the past twenty years. Based on his personal and professional experiences and research, he created the *Seeing True™* transformational philosophy, which has helped thousands of people to clearly identify inner obstructions that impede success. His *Seeing True* approach to dispelling illusions and achieving clarity helps businesses and organizations as well as individuals.

An inspirational and motivational speaker, Chapman shows how seeing differently can produce extraordinary changes to realize human and organizational potential. He is a masterful facilitator who intuitively changes direction based on the needs of the client or audience, as they emerge. In recognition of these exceptional speaking skills, Toastmasters International awarded him the prestigious International Accredited Speaker designation, currently carried by only 58 people worldwide.

Chapman is the author of *What a Wonderful World: Seeing Through New Eyes* (Pagefree Publishing, 2004), a personal growth book/journal with heartfelt stories that celebrate and encourage personal awakening and wonder. He also produced three audio CDs: *Yes – It is a Wonderful World!* (2004), *Seeing True – The Way of Success in Leadership* (2005) and *Seeing True – The Way of Spirit* (2005).

The founder and principal of Magnetic North LLC (www.magneticnorthllc.com), Chapman's consulting practice fosters organization development, strategic planning, and personal and professional growth in public, private and nonprofit organizations. His services include planning, facilitation, leadership and management development, teambuilding, coaching, and training.

Chapman holds a Masters of Social Welfare from the University at Albany (New York), and a Bachelors of Business Administration from Valparaiso University. He also brings a strong background in financial and systems management from a 10-year career with General Electric. He has been an active, award-winning member of Toastmasters International and a national award-winning radio commentator and producer since 1995.

Clients in the United States and internationally have included the World Health Organization, Habitat for Humanity, the Centers for Disease Control and Prevention, Chevron, HealthSouth Corporation, the American Cancer Society, Blue Cross Blue Shield of New Mexico, Regence Blue Cross Blue Shield of Oregon, Departments of Health for New Mexico, Idaho, and New Hampshire, and Texas Tech University.

All profits from the sale of *Seeing True: Ninety Contemplations in Ninety Days* will benefit Holistic Management International (www.holisticmanagement.org), a worldwide nonprofit that helps people heal damaged lands and achieve economic, environmental, and social sustainability. Chapman was the organization's Chairman of the Board from 2004 to 2007.

"Ron has style, grace, wit, sincerity, humor and compassion. To say he is a riveting speaker is an understatement." – Donna Labatt, Toastmasters International 2000-2002 International Director